Bed and Breakfast Magic!
How to Transform Your Bed and Breakfast Into A Booming 6 Figure Business

Yvonne Halling

DEDICATION

This book is dedicated to all our wonderful guests who've stayed with us, referred their friends and families and written fabulous reviews for us on Trip Advisor.

We couldn't have done it without you, and I thank you from the bottom of my heart. X

Yvonne Halling

CONTENTS

Yvonne Halling

ACKNOWLEDGMENTS

Firstly I want to acknowledge Alicia Dunams for her "Bestseller in a Weekend Bootcamp" without which this book would never have seen the light of day. Secondly, I want to acknowledge Rachel Elnaugh and Marie o'Riordan for their contributions to this book. I also want to acknowledge my team, Marion Ryan for her amazing technical expertise, Tony and Nicki Vee for their outstanding business and coaching skills, Lenna Kay for transcribing at ATS Transcription Services and all the partners who've worked on and contributed to the publishing of this book.

Thank you

x

ABOUT ME

My name is Yvonne Halling and I'm the Author of this book. I run "Les Molyneux" Luxury Bed and Breakfast in the heart of the Champagne region of France. You can see us here:
http://bedandbreakfastinchampagne.com

I took this business from almost nothing to making 100k in less than 3 years, and I now help Bed & Breakfast owners worldwide to create a six figure Bed & Breakfast business so that they can have more money, more fun and serve more people.

Why did I write this book?

When I opened my Bed & Breakfast business back in 2001 it was just a "hobby" business, extra money for luxuries while my husband worked full time at Moet et Chandon, the big champagne company.

He was travelling overseas extensively and I needed to have something to do while he was away and I was home taking care of our two daughters, so I opened a B&B. I found that I loved it and the whole family loved it too. It ticked all my boxes.

Among my many skills, I am an Interior Designer and Soft Furnisher. So having a Bed & Breakfast business gave me the opportunity to use those skills on the décor and design of my home. I also love cooking, so preparing meals for guests was rewarding too, and having conversations with interesting people from all around the world ticked the box of meeting new people.

As the years rolled by the girls grew up and circumstances changed, I found myself in the position of having to support my family with a B&B business that was really just a hobby.

At that time I was making around €10,000 a year which was clearly not enough to support us, and so something had to change. It was a daunting task to make a humble Bed & Breakfast hobby business big enough to support us, but there was nothing else to be done and so I set about it.

In my first year I quadrupled that business and in the following year I doubled it again, and now consistently make around €100,000 a year. We have eight revenue streams, a core community of champagne lovers and returning guests. We keep in regular contact with our past guests through blogging and newsletters. Using automated online technology, we "prep" our incoming guests on the services and experiences they can expect when they stay with us. And we now have a business that supports us all.

It has been an exhilarating journey with many ups and downs, and this book is about what I learned. I hope you find it useful too.

When researching for this book, I found that the average B&B is making around 18,000 a year with over half making less than 10,000. I have to confess I was shocked, but not surprised, when I looked around my local area and saw how others were running their B&B businesses. Sadly, not that well.

And I'm not just talking about the old-fashioned décor, the tired bathrooms, the worn out sheets and scratchy towels, the chipped crockery and the often indifference of the owners. I'm talking about the lack of sales and marketing skills and knowing how to attract and take care of guests.

Since opening my B&B in 2001 the landscape has changed completely. No longer do we have to take all-comers, discount our prices, be at the mercy of late arrivals or no-shows, and rely on 3rd party organizations such as our local tourist office or even large travel sites. No, we can take control.

My vision is to have B&Bs around the world, serving their own particular and unique niches with guests who love what they do and have, return again and again with their friends and family and "advocate" because they want to.

To have B&B owners "be somebody" for their guests, sharing their unique expertise and knowledge with people who are interested and turning that into developing additional products and services to better serve that niche, and increase their own turnover and profits.

To create our own economies, independent of large booking engines or so-called 3rd party marketing machines that don't bring us guests we love, and all too often don't bring us any guests at all, but still maintain their high fees.

To raise the standard of the B&B world so that it is recognized as the personal service niche that it is, but is responding to guests' needs, wants and desires in perfect harmony.

To increase the average income of B&Bs to at least 20,000 GBP / 25,000 euros/30,000 US $ per room.

I hope you will join me.

As we go through the book together, you will notice that I have included the opportunity to book a FREE Consultation with me, so please do take advantage of that here: http://bedandbreakfastcoach.com/your-free-bonus/#

On the call, I take you through my 10 Step Diagnostic, which shows you exactly where you are on a scale of 1-10 in each area of your B&B business.

I hope you'll take advantage of this opportunity. I'm looking forward to assisting you.

CHAPTER 1 MINDSET AND BOUNDARIES

Let me explain what I mean by 'Mindset'.

Have you ever noticed the normal conversations around many people, what they talk about; what's in their minds, thoughts; and then their words? This subject fascinates me and I'm constantly listening for what other people say, because I know that what they say is an expression of what they're habitually thinking.

This may sound glib but it's really fascinating if you listen. I saw this phrase once, probably on Facebook, and it made me think, *small minds talk about people; mediocre minds talk about events; great minds talk about ideas.* Here's some ideas based on my own thoughts.

There are two types of people in the world. There are 'wannabe' successful people, and there are 'will be' successful people. Here's what I've observed about 'wannabe' successful people.

- They make excuses and blame the economy.
- They think it's all right for them but, "It won't work for me, I'm different."
- They are afraid to learn new things
- They don't invest in themselves
- They don't invest in their businesses
- They don't take action
- They think in terms of cost and are afraid to change.

And now the characteristics of 'will be' successful people:

- They take responsibility and make their own economy. They think that, "If this worked for someone else it will work for me."
- They embrace lifelong learning.
- They know that constant investment in their own personal and professional development is the only way to achieve success.
- They invest in their businesses consistently and measure results.
- They take massive action.
- They think in terms of return on investment rather than cost.
- They are also afraid to change but they know that changing will bring about better results and they make the changes anyway.

Which group are you part of? I'm serious here. How are you thinking?

Why is it important to understand our own thoughts?

"Thoughts become things, choose the good ones." That's a quote from Mike Dooley who wrote several books; the most famous one being Notes from the Universe.

Science has now proven that thoughts do actually carry a frequency of energy that materializes into the physical. Think about it. When have you consistently thought about something, or worse still, worried about something happening and then it happened? This has certainly happened to me and I'm sure it has to you too.

If you're like me you have habitual thinking patterns which reoccur time and time again. You probably don't even know what they are because you're not aware of them. But here's how to find out what they are.

When faced with a new situation or a decision making process, just observe what comes up for you; observe the thoughts that appear in your head. Those are the thoughts that come up habitually time after time and those thoughts keep you in the same place unless you consciously change them.

Changing your thoughts is not an easy thing to do. Let's not underestimate the power of your thoughts. But it can be done with patience and a little time.

Here's the thing: in order to get different results in your life and in your Bed & Breakfast business, we need to develop new ways of thinking, because our current thinking patterns have got us to exactly where we are right now. Change always begins in the mind so this is important work to be done.

What is the significance of success energy?

As I explained earlier, your thoughts have an 'energy' to them. What does that mean? Well, when you're thinking something negative, those around you can feel it. They sense it, particularly if you consistently think negative thoughts. The negative energy then permeates your environment, and again people sense that; they won't be able to express what they feel, they will just get a sense of it.

Energy is everywhere, all around us, and our personal energy affects our environment. Positive energy can also be felt by those around us, and again, unable to express it, people will have a sense of the positive energy and that of our environment.

So in terms of our Bed & Breakfast businesses it is important for us to be emitting positive energy as much as possible. This creates a positive environment that people can feel. A positive energetic environment will attract positive energetic guests who will feel extremely comfortable staying with you. You will never have any trouble with these guests because they are a perfect match for your own positive energy.

On the other hand a negative energetic environment will attract negative energetic guests who will take out their frustrations and negative behaviour on you. These guests will be problematic, but again, they will be a perfect match for you.

Why do I need to raise my self-esteem?

To create this positive energetic environment we need to focus on our inner worlds. Our inner worlds are made up of our thoughts, beliefs, and emotions, based on our childhood experiences.

If we were nurtured and loved and well cared for in childhood then we will think well of ourselves. But a perfect childhood is unfortunately not the norm in our society. So most of us are carrying around excess baggage of resentment, anger, hate, blame, and consequently do not think much of ourselves. This causes low self-esteem, low expectations of self and life, and poor relationships.

What can be done about that? Being aware of our own self-esteem is the first step.

How can I raise my self-esteem and change my energy?

Becoming aware of our thinking patterns will shine a light on our issues. Here's a process to get started:

Find a comfortable space for yourself where you will not be disturbed. Have a notepad and pencil ready to write down anything you feel. Remember: a negative situation which occurred when you were a child. Feel the emotions you felt back then. Go with the feelings and then let them out without judgment of yourself. Allow those feelings to flow out of you by whatever means you feel are right.

If you need to cry then cry. If you need to punch someone then punch a cushion. Keep going until you feel the energy no more; the emotion no more. Repeat to yourself an affirmation that affirms you and approves of you just the way you are. Make up your own affirmations and repeat them to yourself as often as you can, but at least twice a day: in the morning when you wake and just before you fall asleep at night.

Do not be critical of yourself when you are going through this process. Be kind and loving towards yourself and know that you can indeed make the changes you need to make.

When we understand how going through this process and doing this work is an essential element to increasing our income, we will feel much more inclined to do this. And then we're ready to put in place some boundaries.

Explain what you mean by boundaries?

When we're living in high self-esteem we no longer allow other people to violate us. Our tolerance level is lower. There are more things that we simply will not tolerate. Here's an example:

Joe and Sharon were completely exhausted when they reached out for help. They had been running their B&B for around 3 years and were ready to give up. They had plenty of guests, but were feeling disconnected from them.

Their business boundaries were loose and often violated by guests because they were completely unaware of them. Check in times were frequently not adhered to, and breakfast was a "come whenever you like" affair. They had lost touch with their family and relationships were suffering.

When we allow our guests to arrive and check out, or have breakfast at their convenience, we are in low self-esteem; unable to state our boundaries for fear of upsetting the guests. When we are in high self-esteem we are not afraid to say when guests can check in, when they must check out, and we decide what time we will serve them breakfast. Always being flexible of course but the boundaries are in place.

It's important for you to set the boundaries; it's your life as well. This is your business and it's your life and you deserve to have a life outside the of Bed & Breakfast business even though your business is in your home.

Here's the secret: People don't respect people who don't respect themselves. It does not make guests happier when we allow them to do what they want to do and make all the decisions, and it certainly doesn't make us happier when we're not happy. And it shows. It leaks out of us and guests feel it. If we state our boundaries then guests will be happier because they know the rules. This is your business, you make the rules and you must not let people violate them.

This doesn't mean that you can't be flexible but the rules are in place and everyone knows it. You will immediately raise your own status in the eyes of your guests and everyone will be happy, especially you, which is the most important thing in your business.

Why do I need to be a salesman?

When we have high self-esteem and when we feel good about ourselves then developing sales skills will be very easy. Many people have a negative impression of salesmanship, conjuring images of sleazy used car salesmen from the sixties trying to sell you a dud. Nothing could be further from the truth.

Selling is helping people to get what they want. When you've established your niche you will know what people want and it's your job to provide that. It could be books, it could be an historic tour of your region, it could be a cooking class; it could be a wine tour, a fishing outing, a walking trek, or a spiritual retreat. Whatever it is, when you've decided on your niche you'll be much more in tune with what your guest wants, instead of guessing because when you get the difference you'll have a firm handle on who your guests are; why they come to your B&B and what they want and need.

However, with your new high self-esteem, you'll find it easy to offer your product and services in a helpful way. Rather than feel like you're pushing and trying to make money because that will never work and will leave you both, you and your guests feeling lousy.

Why do I need to have a cancellation policy?

When guests cancel, you need to make a policy around this; you need to decide at what point would it be okay for you to be able to sell the room that they just cancelled. At what point would you need to take the deposit from them and keep it? At what point would you need to charge them for the whole room? This is all about setting your boundaries because when you're setting your own boundaries, you're in control of your own business which is where you need to be because it's your business.

Why do I need to have any policies at all?

It sets out the shop, if you like; it sets out the store for your business. This is what you can do here, this is what you can expect and guests feel comfortable when they know what they're going to have when they arrive. Many, many people running Bed & Breakfast businesses are making less than €10,000 a year which is one reason why I'm writing this book. Because they don't realize that they have control over their businesses.

It's up to you to set the store out and say what you will or will not tolerate in order for guests to feel comfortable when they arrive. That will raise your status in the eyes of your guests. It will increase your bottom line and it will make altogether a happier experience when you are around your guests.

In my own B&B, my check in times are 5pm – 7pm and check out is 10.30am. Between the hours of 1pm and 4.30pm is my own personal time. I can have a nap, read, walk my dog, sun-bathe, go out. I choose because it's my time, and to make sure I'm not disturbed, I hang a sign outside saying that I'm out and will be delighted to welcome them between 5pm and 7pm. I still hang this sign up even when I'm not out, because my time is my time and I deserve to have it.

When it's time to welcome guests, I am refreshed and ready with a smile and I can focus 100% on them and their needs. It's a win/win all round.

I go into this in a lot more detail in the Free Consultation, so please do book your slot here: http://bedandbreakfastcoach.com/your-free-bonus/#

Action steps:

- Spend some time observing your thoughts and start to question what you're thinking. Have some fun with this!

- Invest in small cards and write some positive affirmations on them and read a couple once in the morning when you awake and before going to sleep at night. Your subconscious mind will do the work while you're sleeping

- Smile a lot and smile more. Always, always give the impression that you're having a great life, and you will

- Never, ever talk about your problems with guests. They have their own problems to worry about, and they don't want to hear about yours.

- Practice having "sales conversations" finding out what guests want that you're not providing at the moment.

- Examine your business and personal boundaries and tighten them up so that you have some free time for yourself every single day, plus take some time off regularly with your family

To illustrate just how important this step is, here's an interview I did with Marie O'Riordan…

Interview with Marie O'Riordan

Founder of Legacy Planeteer™ & Honorary Award Winning Philanthropist, Founder of The Forever Method.™ Generations Of Success In Your Lifetime.™

Q   Marie, what do you see are the biggest challenges facing small businesses today?

A: Well I do work with them as well as the larger businesses and you probably saw we made a top new story on CBS Money Watch, ABC, FOX, NBC, and Business and Leadership this week, and that was with a start-up company.

We took them from basically ground zero to six figures in seven days. It was the same, I guess, issues and difficulties they were having, as the question you've just asked for me. I believe it was that they weren't really seeing the wood from the trees, not seeing the expertise that they had built up for years and years and years and years; and they didn't know how to put themselves out there in a way the people understood it. The corporate, technical, advertising speak, equals zero sales.

So we basically humanized them and made them relate to another human being, and they did six figures in seven days, and did more than their entire previous year in a week.

It was fun. It was a fun process and great people.

Q: You've hit upon that humanizing thing really where you're right - corporate speak and advertising, and technical stuff; it does equal zero sales really and you've got to get the emotional connection, I think, with your ideal prospects. With the person who's going to love what you have and then connect emotionally with that person and help them.

Would you agree?

A: And its more than that too because the added important and secret and vital ingredient is that you actually can deliver what you're talking about, that you know what you're doing, that you genuinely can be there for people, provide a solution. So I think the biggest thing right now is actually providing a solution that people need, but they may not have needed yet.

Q: Do you think the challenges have changed or evolved over the years, or do you think they stayed the same?

A: I think we're certainly evolving all the time, every day, every hour, when it comes to technology in particular. I think a lot of the universal themes have stayed the same over the generations; the importance of an individual feeling that they are doing something to help others themselves, their business, but also most importantly is to help other people and their families.

So I think a lot of the universal themes are there. What I think has become very apparent is that what was working pre 2008 isn't working right now; and this was just the grab and go, and it was a queue of people coming in; they didn't care, customer service was dreadful. And it still is in many cases, however you can turn that around pretty quickly when you genuinely have something that can be of benefit to people.

But yes it has changed since the boom. I think this recession has been a gift because it's got people back to basics to realize what's really important to see that actually you are more than your job even if you don't have that anymore. You are more than your salary; you are more than just a number; you are more than just a punch-in and punch-out card.

So I believe the recession has been very good for humanizing; I use that word and I used that word earlier. Humanizing business. And it's put everyone on a level playing field because, okay sure, we work with Fortune 500 companies as well. But we took a business that was 36 years in business and they did $1.335 million in 17 days after working with us and our methods.

So it's working out for a start-up doing six figures in seven days, a 36 year old business - seven figures, 17 days. And then we work with the bigger boys, (there's a non-disclosure agreement so I can't talk about those), but let's just say some of them turnover 65 billion dollars per year.

Q: In your experience Marie, how would you describe small businesses affect and impact the local community?

A: I think it's really great. It's almost like the best infection and virus you'll ever see, because that enthusiasm does actually spread and It's like, "Oh yeah," when you're in a local community and its how people talk about you, when they even think about your name. So you know if I was in Champagne right now and I was to ask some of your neighbors, or some people in the local communities or in the domains: "How does it make you feel when you hear the name Yvonne Halling?" I already know. Their face is going to light up; they're going to speak about you positively.

And that's the impact that someone like you can have in a community setting. So positivity spreads. And to me the key is how someone makes you feel when you even hear their name. That's the key.

Q: Why do you think it's important that small businesses grow?

A: Well it's important for all of us to grow. I just became a brand new Aunty. My brother and his wife have had a little new born baby girl, Grace. It's important for her to grow every day; it's part of life. Evolution. The strap line for business, the forever method is: generations of success in your lifetime.

This is the one thing we cannot stop; its evolution. Its every cell in your body and every cell in your business is just expanding and renewing anyway, so you might as well be in the mindset that growth is a good thing. I think it's essential for everyone to feel that they're achieving something, to be appreciated.

That's where the keys to customer service come true because we all want to be respected. It doesn't matter what country you're in, what language you speak, what color your skin is. To me, it doesn't really matter. Everyone has a deep down DNA belief that they are worth more. And I'm not just talking about money. I'll be honest with you: there are people contact us every day to work with us. We don't because they're only focused on the money.

If someone is completely, genuinely, ethically focused on helping more people; that's going to follow anyway. So to me the focus is always grow but in the right way; and it goes very, very deep in people.

Q: I think it's important to kind of feel like you're increasing your life and giving the feeling of increase every day, to those around you and also for yourself, to feel like you're kind of moving forward. Because one of the great Philosopher's says: "You're either growing or you're dying". You can't stand still, nothing in nature stands still does it?

A: There's no in-between. I find it funny and I jest with people who are in that comfort zone. They're kind of thinking, "Should I stay or should I go?" And you can only encourage them to take that leap of faith or fate, or whatever it is, whatever people believe in. I always choose to believe that whatever it is there's something greater than all of us; whatever that is. And it always scares me when people tell me they have nothing to believe in, because then they don't even believe in themselves and can you work with people like that? I'm not so sure.

Q: No, no, you can't; and that's a great pity. It's a great pity if people don't believe in themselves. Can you share with us Marie, what you believe are the steps to follow when you decide to actually grow a small business, when you decide to get out of your comfort zone. What are the steps do you believe that people should take?

A: I think discipline is very important, but more than that, it's not just clearing out your mind of the negativity. But it's also a physical clear out. One of the first things we do when we go into business is hire a skip. So it's a *de-clutter*, a de-clutter of the mind of the negative talk, of the negative language patterns that we pick up on straight away. And it's also a de-clutter, getting rid of the stuff you don't need.

We were in a business recently and I asked the

question: "Why are there eight scotch-tape dispensers stuck in one part of the drawer? Why are there seven staplers on top of that printer cluttering up the place and there's no staples in any of them? Why is that, tens of thousands of euro/dollars, printers, lying in the corner, in the way when people come through the front door?"

These are the little things that can make a huge difference. So *de-clutter*, it's to make the environment as streamlined as possible, as clean - I'm not saying clinical. I don't believe in the clinical sterile environment, I believe in streamlining which is very, very different. When you do that you actually physically feel better. And when you get rid of the junk, the physical junk and the mental junk; that's the first step we need to be able to take.

They do challenge people because they do have to get out of a comfort zone and move forward very quickly, because we move very quickly. And the one thing our clients always say is: "It's happening so fast". Well I say, "Hang on, it's a rollercoaster baby!"

You've seen someone in the news this week. They trusted us. I mean we just said, "You better hang on for dear life here," and they went with it so it was good.

Q: It's great to work with people like that isn't it, who are actually up for it because they're actually ready to do it

A: Yes, it's fun. And after this I've got a radio show interview about that, this week's success, after this; so that'll be fun as well. To just share this with more people and you know the purpose of this for me with you, is to hopefully inspire and encourage people, or to light a little spark somewhere in their subconscious mind and think, "Yes, there is more to me. I'm not who I am and where I am right now. There is more and there's always the future."

So yeah, if you can ignite little sparks all over the place, you'd be surprised what sort of fires you start - in a good way.

Q: Absolutely Marie. And that's exactly what you did for me a couple of years ago.   You lit that spark for me when I met you in Paris; and I've never forgotten that moment when I just thought: "Hmm, there is more to me than this." It was incredible.

A: I remember that too. I mean you went on to double and then another year you went onto quadruple. You were a headline person to work and collaborate with. It's funny because no matter where the team and I, where we travel; we'd be kind of, "Oh yeah, and there was Yvonne in Champagne in France," and its just - you know we're very proud of you. I know that, even if we don't physically see you all the time, or on Skype; we're very, very proud of what you've done and achieved.

Q: Thank you.

A: And the community that you've created.

Q: Well, as I just said, you ain't seen nothing yet.

A: Yes! there's the attitude!

Q: Marie, what advice would you give to a small bed and breakfast owner who feels that spark, who you've lit that spark in them. What advice would you give to them now that they've decided that they want to go for it; they want to grow?

A: Well something they can do absolutely right now, is

just start listening to what is going on with the voice in their head? Is the voice in their head saying, "Ooh, this is scary?" Or is the voice in the head saying, "Ooh, mm, I think I can do this." And once you can get rid of the negative speak and think, "Yeah actually I can do this." The next thing, you have a physical building where people are staying; and I would say do a de-clutter of your mind and then get a trailer, get something, get a skip and clear out the place.

Get rid of everything unnecessary; not to make it sterile, but to make it even more homely because people love room to move around; and make it feel like their space. So I would say you can do a physical streamlining for this sort of business and industry, immediately. And you'd be surprised how it makes you feel, but more importantly, how it makes your guests feel. And they feel that they have space and room to make this really their home while they're with you.

And I just think positivity in every way. It's the basic stuff, you're the expert not me, when it comes to the bed and breakfast. But what is the simple stuff the universal teams - making people feel great and welcomed. They have an opportunity to spread the word for you; and you know the power of referral business. And you're someone as well who has taken this to the internet and it has spread; and you've taken this to even iPhone or Apps, or applications you can download and that kind of thing.

So you took the lead from the physical to the virtual world and made that a success. And congratulations, I mean you're a new Author now, again, and I'm so proud of you for that. So, if Yvonne can do it, I believe someone who has the talent or authority and has a quality of service already - can just go for it. As we sit here and say 'what's the story like'? Just go for it.

Q: Absolutely, and thank you.

Is there anything else you'd like to say Marie, about business in general; life in general, your philosophy; anything tips and info, insights that you could share?

A: Yeah, what I always find is when someone is prepared to step up to the mark or step into bigger shoes and live the life that they were born to live; because I believe there's a path laid out for everyone. Whether you choose to believe it or not, I feel there's greatness in everyone; its just tapping into it.

What you will find is, as soon as you want to be better, be more; sometimes the people closest to you in your life, will have most resistance. And even the other day we said to a client's husband (and very sternly we said this; it was almost in jest, but we did say very sternly): "You better get used to having a successful life."

And sometimes the people closest to you are afraid, "Oh, oh, what if, what if, what if?" The most negativity will be from the people closest to you and you've got to find a way to deal with that and just go on anyway. And I don't mean to steamroll them, but then again I do.

Q: So what are your plans now for the future? What are you up to, where can we see you?

A: It's been exceptionally busy and we're very blessed. I mean this month alone we're working like crazy to be honest with you, but we've got six cities abroad this month alone; which is always fun. Yeah, just upping the levels. As you know we volunteer a lot and we're working through Planeteers Philanthropy; a lot of charity work.

So we've been giving back to some very, very special people, in Ireland and abroad. So we're really, really enjoying that. And we're upping the levels as well. There's some very exciting people that we're connected with at the moment. I'm hoping within the next couple of months we'll be able to make some of that public.

We're also deciding to do something a little bit crazy, and you know Yvonne, when I get a crazy idea its always an interesting experience. And we're upping the game. We're doing something this year that is going to challenge perceptions of what's possible for business; Gerry's the guy who did 1.335 million dollars in 17 days after our methods.

How that started was, I was on the plane home, to Europe from Oprah. It was the second flight, it was the connecting flight, but it was the main flight. I remember, and I'm quite an unusual personality type and have a lot of flashes or ideas, and crazy ideas every day.

I had a crazy idea and I was flying home after Oprah, and I said, in my head and then I said out loud of course on National Radio when I landed, which was interesting, 'cause then you kind of nail yourself to the cross - you got to do it.

But that thought that flashed into my head on the way back from Oprah on the plane was: "Wow, imagine if I could help make an Irish family business a million a month." And they did 1.335 million in 17 days, and I didn't ask for a penny of that. They kept every cent. The same with David, he's done six figures in seven days; he gets to keep all of that, every penny.

That's how I like to do business - set people up for success.

I've got a really crazy idea that I've had. Actually yesterday while we were driving back from working with amazing people who actually did 1.167 billion dollars in business in New York City. That was very exciting for us. On the way back (we were away for a number of days and travelled back yesterday); and I had this crazy idea. We're going to roll it out at some point this year, very strategically.

I mean, it's all about stepping into bigger shoes too; and we're going to put it out there and see what happens. But there will be positive intent and a true desire to help more people with this; and I feel when you come from that sort of place that everything is possible.

Q: Totally. Somebody said something to me once, a few years ago: "When you're thinking about your client's you've got to love them so much that they feel like they can do anything with you." And I keep that in my head all the time.

A: That's great.

Q: It's about just valuing people so much that they feel so safe with you that they feel like they can do anything with you. And obviously you're having that effect on your clients.

A: Well the other side of it is, as you probably know we did a National TV show recently and it was amazingly positive. Everything just went nuts, I mean, you know the offices - the phones were ringing non-stop 24/7. We couldn't even get a line out to make a call. It was nuts.

But the thing is, you see what people don't realize is, we actually (I mean this with the right intention); we actually turn away 90-95 percent, maybe sometimes 99 percent of everyone who contacts us. Because we've got to be very careful about who we align with. They have to be the right sort of person to want to help other people. And when people see the figures and the financial success, we don't ever want them to get the wrong idea, because it's great when that happens but it's not why we do what we do. And anyone who just rings us up and say, "I want to make a million in a month." "Bye-bye, we're not for you, see ya."

Q: It's not really about the money, it's about what you can do with it; it's about how you can help more people.

A: Yes. That's the difference in this economy, the recession has been a gift, that we've gotten back to basics; and the pure people of good intention are going to thrive, survive and grow right now.

Q: Marie, where can we get you?

A: www.theforevermethod.com is the main website. We always invite people to take a look, see what's going on. If they feel inspired to touch base with us. But as I always say to people: "There's no guarantee we're going to work with them."

Q: No, of course not. Thank you so much Marie. I really appreciate you taking the time to speak with me today. Its lovely to see you.

A: Thank you.

Q: I hope that our paths will cross again soon. Thank you.

A: I hope so. Well, you know this isn't about me; this is

about you and your community and I'm very proud of you, and hand on my heart. She's one of the good ones.

CHAPTER 2 : BUILD A TEAM

Why are people reluctant to hire other people?

The problem with hiring people is possibly affected by our childhood experiences. If your mother did everything herself, the chances are you will think that's how it needs to be done.

Many B&B owners in South Africa, for example, are used to hiring staff; it's what they do. They understand that they have a duty to employ others otherwise if we all did everything ourselves no one would have any work.

There are many reasons for not hiring people, and I've probably heard them all! But in reality, they are just excuses born out of fear.

Why is it important to become an employer?

Business owners hire others to share the workload. If you are a serious Bed & Breakfast owner then you will do the same.

Several years ago, we spent some time living in Japan. In fact our two daughters were born in Tokyo. At that time I got to know several new mothers just like myself and many, if not all, had employed Filipinas to look after their children, clean their houses and do general babysitting. When I first experienced this, I was shocked. I had never employed a cleaner in my life and no one was going to look after my children.

But then a friend explained to me that as a relatively wealthy ex-pat living in Japan, it was our duty to help the Filipinas who had left their homeland in search of well paid work in Japan. One Filipina who was working for my friend had spent several years in Japan and during that time had educated her four children back home; put them all through University and built a house for her retirement.

None of that would have been possible if she hadn't found employment with people like us. I changed my perspective after that and hired a Filipina. It was a joy to have her help with the children and to know that I was doing my part to help her.

What tasks do I need to have someone else do?

When I first opened my B&B back in 2001, I did everything myself and at that time I only had two rooms and the cleaning, washing, ironing, breakfast making, dinner, cooking etc., was just part of the job. I was doing all this for my young family anyway so another couple of extra rooms didn't seem too much to cope with. But back then it was just a hobby business, not a real business.

Then when circumstances changed, I now had four rooms, and things completely changed. To begin with I still managed everything myself but I was becoming exhausted. Not just with the regular cleaning but with the fact that I had to do the marketing now as filling four rooms was more difficult back then than just filling two and I had to fill four rooms as often as possible.

I was at the end of my tether and so I went in search of a cleaner. Two young local girls turned up and I realized in that moment that I needed to help them both by employing them both. They were unemployed and unlikely to be able to get jobs so it was down to me to help them.

That's what real business owners do; they help the local community by employing local people. The penny had definitely dropped. Those girls are still with me, five years on and I couldn't do without them and I let them know as often as I can.

What is my role in my B&B business?

Here's a list of tasks that need doing daily in a B&B business. You can probably add more yourself:

- Meeting and greeting and chatting with guests (Service delivery)
- Preparing breakfast
- ~~Preparing dinner~~
- Cleaning the rooms
- Laundry
- Shopping
- Meal planning
- Gardening/yard work
- Marketing
- Care and nurturing of past guests
- Care and nurturing of incoming guests
- Inventory (stocks of toiletries and foodstuffs)
- Bookkeeping
- Answering enquiries by email or telephone
- Taking bookings by email or telephone
- Developing relationships with local partners
- Identifying local interesting experiences for your guests
- House maintenance.

I'm sure you can think of more but here's the thing; there are only two things that you yourself need to be doing from this list on a daily basis and a couple of things you must do a couple of times a year. From the daily tasks; welcoming guests, i.e., service delivery and getting more guests, i.e., marketing.

These are the most important tasks in your B&B business. Making sure that your guests are having a great experience; only you can do this. Making sure that you have a consistent flow of guests coming; marketing.

Twice annual tasks; developing relationships with local partners and identifying local interesting experiences for guests. Everything else can be done by someone else. What's more if you try to do everything else then you will become exhausted. The tasks are too numerous. Instead, focus on getting really good at your tasks and look around for someone else to do the others. Your job then becomes to manage instead of do.

How do I find good help?

So now you've decided it's time to stop doing everything yourself and now you need to find some help. This can be daunting if you've never employed anyone before and there could be a tendency to think that you won't find anyone who can do (task) as well as you and therefore it's not worth looking.

There are good people everywhere and at the time of writing, many of those good people can't find jobs. Many B&B owners I work with say they can't afford help or they tried it and it didn't work. So let's examine these beliefs here:

"I can't afford help" - If you take the time to work out how much time you spend on tasks that could be done by someone else and then multiply the number of hours you're doing by your hourly rate, you'll see how much you're spending on yourself.

"I prefer to do all the cleaning myself because other people don't do it as well as me".

This is just another common belief because anybody can be trained to do the work that you do. Cleaning's not a difficult task; it just requires some procedures and some guidelines.

If you take a moment to just scope out the cleaning that you like to have done, how you like it done and how often you want it done, then you can train somebody else to do this work just as well as you can. Probably even better because that's their sole job.

Now getting back to the example I cited earlier about spending time on cleaning yourself. If you spend four hours a day cleaning your rooms and your house, and your hourly rate is $50 an hour. Then you're spending $200 a day by hiring yourself. So if you can find someone else who's happy to do that job for you under your guidance and training and you need to pay them $15 an hour, then you've actually saved yourself a $140 a day.

Plus now that you've freed up your time during those two hours, what could you do that will bring you even more money? More than the $200 you would have spent on hiring yourself to do the rooms. Do you see how it's false economy to do everything yourself?

be done by someone else.

.

Bed and Breakfast owners often come to me when they are at the end of their rope and don't know which way to turn. One of the first things I do is examine their thinking about hiring others.
This can be a great stumbling block. They always want to

make more money and I show them how easy it is to do this, but the paradox is that they will not be able to generate more money until they hire someone else, at least part time, or outsource some of the tasks like laundry to other specialists.

Chris and Carol came to me because they were completely exhausted with their Bed & Breakfast business. They had bought their business three years previously from a previous owner and it was already a working Bed & Breakfast and so they didn't really make any changes; they just took over where the previous owner had left off. The irony is that the previous owner probably sold the business because he was burnt out with frustration and exhaustion but of course he didn't say that in the sales particulars!

They came to me and they said, "We're so tired and frustrated with our business, what should we do? What could we do?" So, the first thing I did was examine their business boundaries and their workload. They were letting guests decide when they arrived and guests were showing up at any hour of the day. They were arriving at 11 in the morning; they were arriving as late as 10pm at night. The B&B owners had no time to themselves, they had no private time for their family and they were letting people make the rules and it had taken a toll on their relationships and their family life.

In addition, they were doing ALL the tasks themselves, sometimes taking all day just to keep up with the laundry.

Which position should I hire for first?

Well, now that you've decided that you're going to, and that it makes economic sense to find help, let's take a look at identifying our team members. One of the first tasks you must employ for is somebody to clean your rooms. This is not your job and should never be.

Next you'll want to think about outsourcing your laundry, again, this is not your job. The laundry service will do a much better job than any domestic washing machine and this task takes you away from your tasks of service delivery and marketing for far too long. Find a local laundry service that will pick up and deliver and give them some business too, they probably need it and they will be grateful for it. Everybody needs more business.

Next, how about finding somebody to take care of the garden or the yard. "But I like gardening." You say, well, great then do some but only in your spare time, don't make it your job. Your garden or yard needs to be looking fabulous all the time. Adding this task to your long list of tasks is only going to add to your stress. Get someone else to do the heavy work and you can potter around and enjoy your garden whenever you have time.

How can I outsource small tasks that I don't like doing?

Another task to outsource is cooking and this is really a thorny subject because you'll probably be saying, "But I like cooking." Well, so do I but when it becomes a daily task it's not so much fun unless you are a chef and food and cooking is your passion. In this case this needs to become your primary activity and you may have to consider hiring someone else to do your marketing and indeed the guest facing service delivery. Start small and build from there.

How does having a team around me actually make me more money?

As I said earlier, once you've identified how much you're costing yourself to employ yourself, doing something like the cleaning, you'll realize that it actually makes more economic sense to employ someone else and for whom you can pay less money. That's how you make more money in your Bed & Breakfast and allows you to focus on the jobs that you must be doing which is the two core activities; marketing and service delivery. You must let someone else do the rest of the jobs. SEE PAGE 36

How is having a team around me actually making my B&B work better for everyone?

It means there's less stress on your shoulders. It means that you have time for yourself each day. It means that you can get really, really good at your jobs and you can leave other people to do their jobs. It means that guests will be properly taken care of when they arrive. It means that your house will always be tidy and clean. It means that the food will always arrive on time. It means that you will always be on top form, in good energy, positive expectations and your B&B will be a renowned place to come to stay.

To find out where you are on a scale of 1-10, please book your Free Consultation with me here: http://bedandbreakfastcoach.com/your-free-bonus/#

CHAPTER 3 : RECORD EVERYTHING

Why do I need to keep records?

When I first started my B&B in 2001, I resisted keeping records. After all, it was only a hobby business so what does it matter? I kept a rough idea for tax purposes only but profit and loss or cashflow, no need for all that. Well you may be thinking the same way about your business too and if you're running a hobby business then perhaps there's no need to keep records. However if you're reading this book, chances are that you're not content with the level of revenue you're generating and you'd like to increase it.

Then you will need to start keeping accurate financial records. A magical thing happens when you start to record your income and expenditure. You start to realize where the money goes and then you can make intelligent decisions on how to allocate the available funds. You might be forgiven for thinking you need expensive software to monitor everything but in reality all you need to be able to use is Microsoft Excel.

What do I need to measure and record?

There are four essential spreadsheets that we need to set up and these will paint a picture of your business and how it is performing against your expectations or your budget and against the previous year.

For the moment, let's keep it really simple

How do I set up my spreadsheets?

Your spreadsheets are income and expenses, weekly bookings, occupancy rates by room and daily cash flow. In this section I will take each one separately and explain what it does for you. We'll need to open Excel spreadsheets and put dates across the chart for each week.

I find that a Bed & Breakfast week works best if it starts on the Monday and ends on a Sunday. Your dates across the top of your columns will give the date of each Sunday of each week and then the total column for each month. A column for the same period in the previous year and an up/down column which is the difference between what you've done this month and the same month last year and a cumulative column to see if your business is growing. A cumulative column calculates your up/down column from each previous month so you have a running total of whether you are up or down on last year's figures.

What is a profit and loss statement?

Your profit and loss statement is a record of how much money you took and how much you've spent during any given week..

Your profit and loss statement is your income and expenses statement. Accountants use profit and loss and I say income and expenses. It's a very important element of your financial recording. It tells you exactly how much business you've done each week, month and year and it compares it to last year so we know whether we're growing or dying.

I like to itemize my revenue streams rather than put them all together as other revenue as then I know exactly what makes me the most money and this leads to better marketing for the future.

Now the expenses need to be itemized down the left hand side of your spreadsheet and you enter every single thing you spend money on to run your business. Try to avoid 'other' as much as possible. The more detail you use the better.

Now you know all your income by room and expenses in as much detail as possible, you now need to create the most important piece of information, the profit or loss by week. By taking your total income for the week and subtracting the total expenses for that week, and the amount you have left is your profit.

You always want to include a row of payments to yourself. This is very important from a psychological point of view. If you're not paying yourself anything at all, it can feel like you're working for nothing and that the business is taking everything. We work hard in our Bed & Breakfast businesses and we need to pay ourselves even if it's only a small amount.

I don't include payments for the home loan or utilities either but you can if you wish; it's up to you. Different countries have different structures for Bed & Breakfast businesses. You have to find what's best for your situation.

Why do I need to record weekly bookings?

Keeping track of bookings taken by channel; that is how the bookings arrive, every week, lets us know how bookings originate. I know that 90% of my bookings come from my online booking system. When you've got this setup you'll know where your bookings are coming from too.

Each booking is one room for one night so if someone books two rooms for three nights, that's six bookings recorded here. I also keep a note of how many I've knowingly had to turn away or referred to another

B&B in my local area. This lets me know if adding another room would be a smart decision. In 2012 I turned away over 200 bookings so I approached my neighbor whose house had been on the market for over a year. We agreed that I would manage her house as she'd already moved away and we split the profit between us.

I knew that I could make this work because of the number of people I turned away. What I don't know is how many people had come to my website looking for accommodation but had been disappointed because rooms were not available. As far as I'm aware there is no way of knowing this. What I do know though is that almost 9000 people visited my website in 2012 and 623 bookings were made. More than likely a lot of people have been disappointed.

What's the significance of occupancy rates?

Occupancy rates tell us which rooms are the most popular. Again, helping us to get a clear picture of how our business works.

Your rooms are identified in the left hand column and your dates are again the Sunday's of each month. At the bottom, there's a row which says 100% occupancy, you enter here the actual number of nights your rooms are available for that week. So, for example, in the first week of January, if I only had ten nights available to sell because I was closed during the first part of the week over the New Year holiday., then I would enter 10 in the availability cell. In the second week, I only had 14 rooms available to sell because two of my rooms were being decorated. In the second and third weeks, I was at full availability and had 28 rooms available to sell each week.

I then had to look at my diary at the end of each week

and enter in the number of nights sold by room which would then automatically calculate in the total row and then automatically calculate my percentage occupancy for the week. Giving me an overall percentage occupancy for the month of January, the totals by month add up for the whole year and then I know how many rooms I sold during the entire year and can compare that to last year as we did in the Profit and Loss statement.

I hope you're still with me.

What is cashflow and how does it work?

Possibly the most important spreadsheet you will ever create and the most illuminating for me personally is the cashflow spreadsheet. Why is that and how does it work? Let me explain. Your cashflow is your daily income and expenses that pass through your bank account and now reconciles to your bank account on a weekly basis. It includes every single transaction that goes through your bank.

It does not include any cash expenses that you fund through the cash in your purse or wallet although the cash taken out of the bank will be recorded on the spreadsheet. If you're worried about too many cash withdrawals and no records of where the money has gone then I recommend keeping a little notebook with you at all times to record those little expenses that seem to drain your cash away. But for the purposes of your B&B business, let's delve into how the cashflow spreadsheet works.

First open the new spreadsheet and instead of putting weekly dates in the top row, as in the other spreadsheets, put daily dates in. Down the left-hand side your income rows will look similar to the profit and loss statement.. We don't need to know which rooms were sold for this spreadsheet. We're only interested in how the money arrives in our bank account and then the total for each day.

Your row underneath your dates will be your carry forward amount from the previous week. Then enter each day the sum of money which landed in your bank account per day. You can record this accurately by using your bank statement at the end of each week by online banking or even daily by using online banking. I do it weekly and then make adjustments from the bank statements at the end of every week.

Next we need to list the expenses in our cashflow spreadsheet and these are the same rows down the left hand side as your profit and loss statement. Enter in each day when these expenses occurred in your bank account. At the bottom you'll have a total expenses per day which then needs to be deducted from your total income per day to leave you with the profit/loss amount. This is the amount that gets carried forward to the top of the column for the next day. If you use formulas which I highly recommend, it will automatically calculate for you.

I also add a row called 'At bank' to make sure that my own calculations correspond with what's in the back account at the end of each week. It keeps things accurate and if there's any discrepancy, I can spot it straight away.

Action Steps:

- If you're not already recording everything I've just talked about, then go to http://bedandbreakfastcoach.com/your-free-bonuses/ to download the spreadsheets, save them to your computer and use them on a weekly basis.

- Make a date to do this at the same time every week and if you feel resistance to doing it, know that this is exactly what you need to get past

- If you're not doing online banking, then sign up for it. It will make record keeping far easier, and you don't want to be waiting until the end of the month to find out how much money you've made or lost. We need to be on top of it weekly.

If you'd like to find out where you are on a scale of 1-10, then book a Free Consultation with me, and I'll take you through the whole process: http://bedandbreakfastcoach.com/your-free-bonus/#

CHAPTER 4: WHO DO YOU WANT TO SERVE?

Why is it important to define your target guests?

Well, let's think about the old paradigm. The old paradigm, it says, "Everyone is my customer." When I first opened my B&B in 2001, I was one of those people that fell in love with the house, spent a fortune on decorations, soft furnishings and accessories and then opened my doors. I'm sure you know people like me and perhaps you even did this too. But don't worry, it's not a crime and back in the dark ages before the internet, this was a pretty good strategy.

We had no way of choosing, segmenting, targeting or marketing to our ideal guests. We had no way of reaching them, again, to invite them to come back and stay with us. There was no way of letting them know about our special deals, special weekends, added value, extras and even what was going on in our local area which could interest them. Times have changed. Have you?

There's a myth running around and you hear it often when you're in business and it goes something like this: Question, who is your ideal customer? Who do you help? Answer, well everyone really, anyone who's blah, blah, blah. This is the old paradigm at work. We think we have to help everyone. We think we have to take anyone. We think that everyone, no matter who, is our customer.

The new paradigm goes like this: People like me.

Since the arrival and the mainstream adoption of the internet, we, as B&B owners now have the power to choose who we want to have in our homes. We can target our marketing to those people. We know more people like them who bring their friends and who buy everything we have because they love us. "But I love the diversity of my guests." I hear you say. Yes and that's a good thing, but ask yourself, how is this working for your bottom line and your stress levels? When we drill down into our own talent, expertise and knowledge and start packaging that knowledge into products and services that people want then you begin a new chapter in your Bed & Breakfast life.

How do I know who my target guests is?

Imagine that you are a keen fisherman. You love fishing; you know all the best places to fish in your local area. You know when it's best to fish for certain fish and when it's not. You know all the local fisherman supplies people. You are part of the local fishing community.

Now imagine another keen fisherman who's coming to your area for the first time, he knows nothing of what you know and so he needs some help. You can help him. You can enthusiastically tell him about all the best places to fish in your local area. Let him in on your insider secrets of where to fish for certain fish and where not to. You can introduce him to the products of your local fisherman supplies people. You can make him feel like part of the local fishing community if only for a short time.

You can also create products and services to meet his needs there by increasing your bottom line while having fun talking about your favourite subject, fishing, to people who want to know.
Do you see how this works?

Why is it important to discover my own expertise and knowledge?
Let's talk some more about your unique skills, expertise and knowledge. You might get caught up in the belief that well, someone else can do that better than me or

someone's already written a book on doing that. It's a common misconception that if someone else is already doing what you are skilled in yourself, then there's no point in you doing it.

Just take a look at how many books, magazines, TV shows there are around cooking. Hundreds right? You may think your new recipe book on your specialist area is not worth writing. Wrong. The people who come to your B&B are looking for an emotional connection with you, otherwise they choose a hotel. After all a bed is just a bed. Don't underestimate the power you have to serve people with your skills, expertise and knowledge; because that's why they choose to stay in a B&B. Your job is to help them meet their needs and you can do that by packaging up your skills, expertise and knowledge, in a way that meets their need for an emotional connection.

How do I do this?

Well let me give you an example. My husband wrote a book on his specialist subject: Champagne. Thousands of books have been written on the subject, but not from his perspective of living and working there for many years. He wrote the book on a Word document, self-published it for free and has sold hundreds of copies in our B&B and on Amazon, a win-win for everyone.

The champagne lovers who come to our B&B have got a emotional connection to my husband and wanted a memory to take away with them and he sold a book. Perfect.

How do I find my target guests?

You probably dismissed your own skills, expertise and

knowledge as, "Oh that…" it's nothing. And by doing that you are dismissing your own value in the world. It's not nothing and it does matter. It's very easy to dismiss our own skills as something unimportant, or to think that everyone knows that; when the truth is that everyone doesn't. And even if they did no-one knows it from your own perspective. Take a look on Amazon and count how many books there are on any subject; there's always more than one and in some categories there are thousands.

They've all written on the same topic but do they all say the same thing, "No." Each is written from the unique perspective of the author and no one can copy that.

When you dig deep and find out what your own field of knowledge and expertise are then I would suggest that you owe it to yourself and the world to share it. I would even go as far as to say that keeping it hidden is selfish.

People want what you have. When they come to your B&B they are looking for your unique take on things; the way you see it. The unique experiences that you can introduce them to because of you.

Even if there are many other people in your local area who seem to know just as much as you, they don't have your unique take on it.

So taking the example I've just shown you, take some time now to think about your own field of expertise and knowledge that is locked inside your head and that you take for granted. You perhaps think that everyone knows what you know, but they don't. We're all totally unique.

Here's a little exercise to get you thinking:
- Why do people come to my area?
- What do I love to talk about?

- What do I love to share?
- What information do I give out over and over again verbally?
- What do I know a lot about?
- What skills do I have that I take for granted?
- What knowledge around those skills have I accumulated over the years that I take for granted?

Take some time to think about these questions. You may uncover many areas of expertise that you didn't realize you had which often happens.

Take a sheet of paper and put each area you've uncovered when going through the questions around each expertise. Don't just dismiss anything that comes up. And if you feel some resistance to doing this exercise then take a little time, but you really do need to do it.

Find a quiet place where you can be alone and get started. And come back to it over and over again whenever you want to add something. Can you see what a totally unique being you are?

Once we've discovered who we can best serve with the knowledge, expertise and skills we have, we have to go out and find them, and the best place to find them is online. They could be in groups on Linked In or Facebook. They could be on Twitter. They could be on the travel forums on Trip Advisor.

Okay so once we've decided on who we want to serve; we have uncovered our skills; we've realized that we know a lot more than we thought we knew about our local area. We then need to check on Google to see who is searching for what we have.

Here's the link to the Google Keyword tool where you can do a little video on this and find people who are looking for you and your B&B and the skills, expertise and knowledge that you have.

https://adwords.google.com/o/Targeting/Explorer?__c=1000000000&__u=1000000000&ideaRequestType=KEY WORD_IDEAS

How important is it that I get on page 1 of Google?

Page 1 of Google is really the very best place to be and it is quite easy to get there once we go through this process that I've just talked about.

You're unlikely to get to number one spot on Google because people pay to be there, big search engines; big companies like booking.com and TripAdvisor pay to be on the top of Google.

But you can definitely get to position four or five on page 1 of Google using the key word tool around your expertise, around your local area, once we've uncovered what it is that you can do so well.

What about people who come that aren't my ideal guests?

We all get people who come that aren't our ideal guests. But as time goes on and you get more and more into this process you'll find that more and more people are showing up who are exactly matched to what you have and what you can offer them.

When people come who aren't your ideal guest, I just give them the same treatment as everybody else and introduce them to what you have. And you may find that they'll become a fan.

But mostly over time people who come to my B&B are coming for the same thing. They're looking to discover the hidden gems of Champagne. And that's because we've managed to position ourselves as the go-to people in that niche in this area.

And you'll be able to do that too in your B&B.

But won't I lose business if I focus on one type of person?

Well the irony of this whole situation is that you'll actually increase your business. And I know that there's a fear of loss here and I know that you could be thinking, "Well I can't just narrow my niche down to these people."

But what happens when you actually hone in and really, really serve that target group of people that we've just uncovered, you will find that you will have a much more enriching experience in your B&B and so will your guests.

And you will find that you'll get more business that way as well because people like people who are like us. And once they've discovered you and they've experienced what you have to offer here, because you're very clear on what it is that you do offer, then they will be more attracted to you and they will tell their friends, who are also like them.

Why does serving a small group of people extremely well mean I can charge more?

Well again the irony of the situation is that you don't need to think about price any more once you've got your target market sorted. Once you've got your niche; you've found your niche; you've uncovered your skills and expertise and you're serving that niche with what you have, you'll be able to charge whatever you like; whatever the market can bear.

And instead of looking around your local area to see what everyone else is charging and positioning yourself somewhere in the middle, then you will be thinking about, "Well I know that I'm getting booked up here; I know that I'm having to turn people away, so therefore I can put my prices up." It's the law of scarcity in fact that comes into play here.

And in your local area there are the most expensive B&B's and there are the cheapest B&B's so somebody's got to be the most expensive, so why couldn't it be you.

So how does defining my target guests mean I will never need to worry about what others in my area are charging?

Well as I've just explained this is where you are building a community of people, like a tribe of people who love what you do and who come again and again because you are completely matched to their needs, wants and desires with what you have.

And so you never have to think about what others are charging because you're not offering the same thing. You're offering a completely different experience. So it's like saying, "Well how can I charge $1 for this apple and $2 for this orange," it's not the same thing. It's filling a completely different need.

So when you've actually got yourself aligned with your target audience and you're offering them a unique experience with you because that's what they're looking for then you won't have to worry about what anyone else is doing because they're not offering the same experience as you are.

When we switched our focus from taking all-comers to finding our ideal guest – champagne lovers worldwide who want to discover the hidden gems of Champagne I quadrupled my business in less than a year.

Action Steps:

- Do the exercise and uncover your knowledge

- Do the keyword research and find out what guests come to your area for and how you can meet their needs in your unique way

- Start thinking about more products and services you can create to serve your new ideal guests. We'll get to that later in the book.

To illustrate the benefits of determining your ideal client, here'san interview I did with Rachel Elnaugh.

INTERVIEW WITH RACHEL ELNAUGH

Rachel Elnaugh, award winning entrepreneur, Creator of the multi million pound market leading experiences company Red Letter Days, when she was just 24. She was also the star of BBC TV's Dragon's Den series I and II. Author of the book Business Nightmares, Creator of Business Alchemy, and award winning business mentor and professional speaker. Last year she co-produced the 12.12.12 One World experience.

Q: So welcome Rachel, thank you so much for agreeing to chat with me today.

So speaking today about how and why it's necessary to define your target market. Can you just give us a bit of background on your thoughts on this issue?

A: Well, the real eye-opener for me was back in my Red Letter Days era; because when I started out in business I had no formal marketing training. I was kind of making it up as I went along so you're kind of testing to see what worked and I think most people approach business like that.

Then a massive step change in the business happened about seven years in when I met one of my first mentors who was a marketeer. He encouraged me to do some formal market research into our business. Now by that point we'd got about a million pound turnover business, so it was a good business. It wasn't huge but it was a very good business by that point. That was when we first started doing proper market research, so moving really through a gut feel where I thought I knew everything there was to know, into being a bit more disciplined about it.

So we did quantitative research. In other words we analyzed our data base of customers to that point, and we also did a lot of qualitative research and we did focus groups, and really started to get to understand what our customers thought.

One of the amazing things that came out of the quantitative research, in analyzing our database was that, in amongst all these people that we'd interacted with, there was this customer. She was an executive wife who lived in a detached house. Her husband was an executive. She drove a Ranger Rover, shopped at Marks & Spencer's, and we called her "Gillian".

So we built up this picture of this woman who was our ideal customer and when we actually started powerfully speaking to Gillian, in everything we did, as opposed to trying to speak to everyone. And this is the big mistake that most people make in business; they try to speak to everyone. And in doing so they kind of dumb down their message because they want to appeal to as many people as possible.

Actually the reverse is far more powerful. When you speak to one core target customer group really powerfully, in their language; and when I say their language I don't just mean words, I mean visual imagery, branding, product creation, content; the whole lot. That is really powerful. And the result in our business was that we went from one million to three million, to five million, to ten, to fourteen, to eighteen million turnover, really fast.

I really got from that the power of understanding your core target customer, and communicating really powerfully to that customer; almost like you're talking to one person. A bit like the intensity of us having a conversation now. It was a huge lesson for me so that's really where it stems from, this idea of powerful communication in marketing.

Q: Why as a small business, is it necessary and important to define your target market? Because resources are much more limited. I mean people who aren't already turning over a million would struggle to do that kind of research. Can you just explain why?

A: That's a bit of a red herring to say, "Oh, we couldn't afford to do the research." At the end of the day it's a mindset and the mindset of most businesses is: "How do I get more business? I know, I'll try and appeal to more people".

And so what happens is, they start trying to be all things to all people; and the problem with that in marketing is it makes your communication the very lowest common denominator because you're having to speak to everyone. For example, if I say to someone, "Who's your target customer?" And they say, "Oh, its women aged 18 to 50." And maybe they're a manufacturer of clothing. If you create clothing; how on earth can you appeal with the exact same clothing and range to a girl aged 18 as well as a woman aged 50? You get what I'm saying?

Q: Yes, absolutely.

A: Now, that doesn't mean at all that, if you speak powerfully to Gillian who happens to be a 38 year old executive wife; that doesn't mean that Sandra who's 24 who aspires to be like Gillian, won't buy it too. However, in creating powerful communication with one target customer, you give your brand and your messaging an intensity which makes it really clear what you're about and that's how you get to stand out from the crowd. Do you see what I mean?

Q: Absolutely. I have the same problem when I mentor, Bed and Breakfast owners; because I ask them, "Who's your target client?" And they say, "Tourists."

A: Yes!

Q: Well that's not specific enough; we have to dig down deeper and get to the gold.

A: Exactly, that's right.

Q: So how would you go about doing that then Rachel? How would you go about deciding who you're going to serve?

A: Well, obviously, a good starting point is who your customers currently are. However, you have to bear in mind that your current customers are a symptom, shall we say, of your current marketing.

So there could be another whole group of customers out there, where you haven't even bothered to target at all. And that's one of the big unknowns in marketing. Its always good to look at what's working and build on that as a starting point.

But I think the thing is, it's really easy in business, particularly when you're a small business and you built it all on your own; is to think you know the answer and to go on gut feeling rather than actually doing some analysis. And the analysis I'm talking about where you can just send your database to a company and have it profiled.

They actually only cost a few hundred pounds. It's well worth that investment because it stops you going on guess work and it moves you into building your business based on some real data and some real understanding. Because the thing to me in business, is that the more knowledge you have the more power it gives you; and so when you're just working on guess work and hunches, that can get you to a certain point but there comes a point when it's really good to start actually doing some proper research. So it doesn't have to be expensive is what I'm saying.

Q: That's very interesting. I think that's well worth doing, particularly if you've got a business that's already going, and as you just demonstrated; even though your business is small, then you have the power of actually homing in on who it is that you're actually appealing to and who would actually love what you have and then buy everything.   It's so much more powerful than marketing to the "white" space and just hoping.

A: Exactly. And this kind of brings us onto the idea of building a "tribe. Another big issue that I often see businesses, particularly start-up businesses is they will create something, and they'll spend a lot of time creating it and putting a lot of energy into it; whether it's a product range or an event, or a new service or a B&B even.

Then after putting all that effort in they will go out to a largely unsuspecting market and try and flog it, and then hit problems because they've got an element wrong. Maybe they got the price point wrong, or if it's an event they've got the day of the week wrong; you know because they kind of guessed at it. And the beauty of having a tribeof follower's, is you can actually ask your tribe what they want.

I'll give you a classic example. Someone came to me for a bit of help and advice; they actually wanted me to get involved in a project. It was a workshop event they were planning to run on, on Saturday November the 5th, and they wanted my help in marketing it. I said, "Well, who are you aiming for?" They said, "Well, it's going be mainly women." I said, "Well, you do know that Saturday November the 5th is Bonfire night (a festival in the UK) and most women who have got a family won't be able to go on a one day event on Bonfire night. You do realize that?"

Now, the person I was speaking to didn't have any children. So what I actually said to her was, "Look, why don't you go out to the tribe of people that you're going to market this to; ask them what their needs are. Ask them what type of event that would be useful to them. Ask them what length of an event would be useful. Would they prefer to do a lunch event, an evening network event, a one day event, a weekend event, a week day. Ask them how much they'd be prepared to pay for this.

It was really interesting because we did a survey, and it came out really powerfully that there were two answers. One was a one day event which was a week day and then there was another set of answers, which was that people would really like a weekend; a whole weekend. And so actually what they formulated was a one day week day event with an up-sell to a full weekend event. So they got the best of both worlds.

But they would never have got to that solution if they had just guessed and just gone for the one day event. They probably wouldn't have got many people there because they'd done it on a Saturday when everyone's busy. And then they probably would have said, "Oh well, we got the price wrong," or "Maybe we got this wrong," or "Maybe we got that wrong." And learning that way through trial and error is very longwinded, very demoralizing and very expensive.

I think it's really powerful to do your research a bit and ask your tribe what they want and then give it to them; there's no better way to build a business than giving people exactly what they ask you for, if you think about it.

Q: No, I totally agree and it's so much easier to do that now, because I was one of those people who created a lovely bed and breakfast business back in 2001, before the internet. We didn't have all these tools that we have now. We didn't even have the internet.

And so, I was one of those people who created a beautiful home, because I love decorating all those soft furnishing things, and then opened my doors. I waited and waited. And that's what people do, I see it a lot.

They don't really know who they're appealing to and they don't really know who they even want to appeal to because, as you say, it's that mentality where you think you have to appeal to everyone.

A: Well, just going back to that point you made Yvonne, there, about - back in the days when there was no internet; and I remember really well, in the very early days - the "Red Letter Days", when we were struggling and nothing was working. But we had fifty customers, just fifty people had bought from us; and that was after a year's trading.

However, I decided to send a different questionnaire which I typed out myself, and I printed on my little Daisy Wheel Printer, in those days we posted out manually. And I got 34 responses and I thought, "Oh that's interesting." And then I had some guy, some consultant from some DTI government funded school, who came in to try and help me with my business.

I told him about this questionnaire. He was a marketing guy and I said, "Oh yeah, I sent this thing. Yeah look, here's all the responses." He says, "Well how many did you get?" I said, "Well 34." "Well, how many did you send?" I said, "Well, 50." He said, "Do you know how much good will you've got in this business?" And I said, "No, isn't that normal to have that kind of response?"

The point I'm trying to make is you don't necessarily have to have internet tools and in the old days, businesses thrived through old fashioned word of mouth. So when you put the power of the internet behind that you can create a phenomenal business really quickly, whereas in the old days it took a decade to do it like I did.

Q: What do you see Rachel are the biggest challenges facing small businesses today then?

A: Well, I would actually say Yvonne; this is a bit metaphysical, but you know I'm very much in that world. Actually, the biggest single challenge is people's mindset; their thinking and belief systems around money. Most people exist in a world very much based on what has happened up to now, and they put all their energy in what has happened up to now and essentially get more of the same.

They don't understand how they're creating a vicious cycle because things go wrong, they give that a lot of energy, more stuff goes wrong, and then before long they're in this very doom and gloom negative cycle. To create a shift in the results you're getting you've really, really got to stop looking at what's happened in the past and really start putting your focus and all of your energy on what you do want and what you want to create. It's what I call "*back from the future thinking*".

So you start creating your present from the future as opposed to building on the past. It sounds a bit weird but it's very powerful when you start putting all your energy on what you do want, and powerful visions of your amazing future. Because very few people, if you think about it unless you're a big daydreamer; very few people put much energy at all onto the future. They put it all onto the past, like what happened, what happened in the past, "Oh I did that once before and it didn't work." "Oh this person's let me down," "Oh, I haven't got enough money, I can't afford that." I mean all these things are based on past events and current reality which is a result of everything that's happened up to now.

The problem is, what you focus your energy on is what you'll get more of, so if you're in that negative cycle of struggling you'll get more struggle. You've really got to start breaking that cycle by shifting all of your focus onto the amazing life you want to create, even if it's not anything like what you've got at the moment.

Q: Especially if it isn't…

A: Which is very counter intuitive because we're taught in a completely different way to that; we're taught completely opposite of that where you've got to sort of have evidence before you'll believe in something you know.

Q: I think it's a very fascinating area. And certainly when I'm mentoring bed and breakfast owners, some of the deepest work or the biggest things that we have to deal with is the mindset.

A: Absolutely.

Q: Getting over the fact that they want to make more

money. Ninety seven percent in a recent survey that I carried out said that they wanted to make more money, but what people don't realize is you can't make any more money if you don't make that shift in your mindset first.

A: Absolutely.

Q: And that was a huge revelation to me; you know when I was earning $10,000 a year.

A: Yes Absolutely. I think the other slight danger area, well it's a big danger area; but most people get drawn into when they're in that trap where they want to make more money. Anyone you ask says, "Oh yeah, yeah, yeah, I want to make more money, I want to be prosperous." But they approach it from this place of how can I make, how can I take? As opposed to what can I give? And energetically the difference between what can I make, what can I take is a million miles opposite to what can I give? What amazing value can I create? Because the more you focus on creating value in my experience, the more money ends up flowing to you because all money comes to you from other people.

So if you are just trying to make more money and kind of take from others it doesn't actually work very powerfully. Most people can sense that you just want their money. So they basically cut costs and scrimp around the edges and make the experience less so they can make more margin. They put their prices up and so they end up giving an inferior product which is more expensive so people don't recommend them and refer them and people don't come back and then they wonder why their business kind of goes down the toilet.

So it's always "how can I make it better? How can I give even better value? How can I make a better experience even more fabulous" and going in that direction which is marketing thinking really as opposed to operational finance control thinking. I had an experience of this. I don't often fly first class, but I flew to Boston first class on British Airways at a time when they were clearly going through a lot of problems about ten years ago I flew first class for one of the first times and it was really obvious that the accountants had got hold of the business. So the accountants, a classic thing, what can we cut? How do we make more money through cutting. Let's cut stuff. So in the toilets of the first class cabin was really cheap scratchy toilet paper. Now most people who travel first class I would imagine, even me in my little home here, I'm used to soft style toilet paper.

So if you're flying first class you expect what you get in a five star hotel. Not the scratchy stuff which you might get in a public toilet. So it's just small things like that that you just think, "Do you know what? I don't know what it was about that British Airways first class experience, but I think next time I'm going to go with Virgin." It's that kind of thinking. You see most things in marketing and business are subliminal, most things in life are subliminal.

So I'm not quite sure what it was about that bed and breakfast but you know what? I don't think I'll re-book this year, I think I'll try the place down the road, you know. So it's that kind of thing whereas the places, the hotels and the bed and breakfasts that have the magic are the ones where people go, "Oh just got to go back there 'cause I want another piece of that magic. I can't say what it was, there's something about that place that's amazing." It's that kind of feeling. It's like the restaurant that you just think, "Oh I've got to go back to that restaurant because there was something magical there."

And when you get that magic going in your business it's incredibly powerful because you get an emotional connection with your customers, they tell everyone, they love it, they rave about it. You've got an advocate and advocates are your biggest unpaid marketing department. So putting a lot of emphasis, I mean we found this in our Red Letter Day era as well. This is another statistic which kind of blew my mind.

No matter how much push advertising we did, so like print advertising and radio ads and even in the time when we were doing TV advertising where we spent about a million pounds on a TV campaign ridiculously. No matter how much of that push stuff we did, eighty-one per cent of our business came from recommendations and referrals.

So if you think about it, if we were spending a million pounds on push advertising, the referral income or that proportion of the business was worth four million pounds in terms of how much we would have had to spend to get that money. So it meant that everything that we put into creating great experiences, that was worth four million pounds. So if you put it into that context of course you should have gorgeous soap in the bathroom and soft toilet roll. Those things don't cost a lot but they make a huge difference psychologically and emotionally to the experience.

I mean it's different I think if you're running a cheap hotel where it's just the cheaper the better. But I think most businesses aren't in that price zone. I mean most businesses can't compete on price actually. They have to compete on some kind of USP which is about magic, that's my experience.

Q: Yes I totally agree with that, I totally agree, and the magic is what we focus here in Champagne and it is subliminal, it is subliminal because we don't focus too much on the flash toiletries. But what we do focus on is emotional care with the customers. That's what they feel. Like you said, you can't quite say what it is.

They'll say they had such a wonderful time but they can't say what it was because it's so emotional and subliminal that they can't even articulate it and I've certainly worked a lot on that over the years and that's what's made the difference. Once I'd got that my thoughts created my reality for a start, and how I'm showing up energetically creates an experience for someone else. Once I understood that I focused a lot on that.

A: Definitely 'cause the thing is you can, it's very easy, especially if you've been running a business for some time, to start resenting clients as a bit of a pain in the butt. That is a massive, massive dangerous place to be. Such as, "Oh no, the people from the upstairs room are at the door again."

Q: Those lovely people who are paying our bills?

A: Exactly, and that's the connection you've always got to preserve and I just think if you can't have that connection with a client or if you've lost your passion for your business you need to get out of the business really. Because how can you create magic if you're in a place of anger or resentment around your business or your clients or whatever you're doing?

Q: And of course one of the things that I focus on with my clients is taking regular time out for yourself so that you replenish. Like you say, fill your tanks.

A: Yes.

Q: You've got to take that time out to fill your own tank 'cause you can't serve anybody when you're exhausted.

A: And I think it's like me experiencing other coaches and see how they do it, and you experiencing other B&B's. I think it's really interesting isn't it? If you run a hotel, experiencing how other hotels do it and kind of being a bit of a magpie for ideas and inspiration from how other people do it and constantly being in that zone of how do I get better? How do I improve? How do others do it? What tricks do they use or tips? What can I learn from other people? And being on a constant quest for brilliance really but that's a very nice place to be and adjusting it around the business of thinking, "Wow how can I make it even better, even better? How can I blow peoples mind?"

Q: What do you see as the opportunities now in business? What would you say to a small business, such as a small bed and breakfast business who wanted to grow. What would be the opportunities for them right now do you think?

A: Well I think in most small businesses, a lot of people complain about the economy, the this and the that and the other, but for most small businesses you don't actually need that many customers to be successful. You don't need a huge amount of market share so actually being in a place of, oh no one's spending money or the economy's down or the tourist industry's down is really not an excuse for anyone.

I think it applies if you've got a huge market, if you're Tesco or someone, then it matters if people stop buying groceries. But usually you are the master of your destiny completely within your sector and there's no reason whatsoever why you can't achieve exactly what you want with your business. I think that's the number one thing and it does come down to the mindset idea because it's so easy to blame isn't it, to blame external factors for the reason you're failing.

So I think once you've taken that on board then I think you have to be really clear about what you do want because the problem is that most desires are a paradox or can create paradoxes. So for example I might want to create lots of money but equally I want to have lots of free time to spend with my family. If you're not careful you can get into this either/or mentality of if I go for the money I'm going to have to sacrifice my freedom. So you've created a mental kind of paradox. So one foot's on the accelerator and other foot's on the brake and then it's quite difficult to get the car to go anywhere.

So it's this idea of moving from these limiting beliefs which is either/or, I can either have this or I can have that, into how can I shape a life that gives me everything I want? So it's about shaping a business which is not just giving you the money you want, it's giving you the freedom you want, it's giving you the joy you want, it's giving you the inspiration you want. I think it's very important to scope a business from a lot of different matrix like that and to work out how you can create a business that gives you everything you want.

So for example with you, you're bringing in someone to help you run the business because you're focusing on coaching and mentoring. So it's kind of thinking through the lifestyle you want to create and how the business sits within that. I don't really see any such thing as a work/life balance, to me it's just my life and what I choose to devote my life to. When you put it in that context and your work is your passion and you give it that kind of energy, that heart energy as you were saying, then everything takes on a new meaning.

When you're a hundred per cent devoted to whatever it is you're doing, even if it's cleaning the toilet. There were times when I had a holiday cottage where my cleaner was away and I would go up there myself with my rubber gloves and bleach and passionately clean the toilets because I wanted it to be great for them, you know.

Q: Yes I do, I understand that totally. Thanks Rachel. Is there anything else you want to say?

A: I just wanted to say one other thing that popped into my mind about this subliminal thing. There's some very practical things and at one time with my holiday cottage the boiler or the thermostat broke down. Basically what it meant was the cottage was very hot upstairs, but downstairs was very cold until I got it fixed. It was really interesting the number of complaints about stupid things that came during that week or two where we had maybe three or four different families or groups coming.

So it wasn't just one particular difficult group; it was across a whole group of people.

The interesting thing that I got from that, is that when people are cold they complain; and so keeping people warm is quite a key thing. Again, it's the subliminal factor, but a really practical one; is that, just by turning the heating up a couple of degrees and getting people nice and warm in a hotel.

I mean, it's equally bad if it's too hot, but generally in England; you know just simple things like that, sometimes it can be the simplest thing that you've overlooked; and you're looking for the complex reason. You can easily be thinking that its all the little things they complained about that were the problem, without realizing that there was another problem over here that you didn't spot.

Which triggered everyone to be unhappy about things they wouldn't normally complain about. So, being a detective and looking for the clues; that's quite an interesting one as well.

Q: That is interesting. This year I put my prices up because I want to be able to offer free champagne to everybody, because people come to Champagne to taste champagne, and so in order for me to offer free champagne I needed to put my prices up. And I find that everything gets better after they've had a glass of champagne.

A: Yes.

Q: That could look like anything really but turning the heating up is a really powerful analogy.

A: Definitely. Yes, and I can totally imagine that… because actually, when I used to drink, champagne was definitely my favorite drink. And you know those events you go to where you get a welcome glass of champagne and then suddenly its dried up and there's no more? Know

Q: A horrible feeling isn't it?

A: It's awful. And just something small like that, which just kind of sends a message of like: 'This is a low budget event', or 'maybe the champagne is just 'Asti Spumante' or something. It's just a small thing; even I notice stuff like that. It makes a big difference I think anyway.

So, the small touches. Lots of small things. I remembered really earlier on in life. Again some marketing course I went on and it really stuck with me, is that they said: "Successful business is about getting a thousand small things right". Because we keep looking for the big splashy idea, the silver bullet that's going to change everything and change our life. But actually getting a thousand small things right consistently over a long period of time can actually take you a lot further than any one big thing. It's just like attention to detail day in, day out, being consistently brilliant; it's actually quite powerful and most people don't get that at all.

Q: No, no they don't. And sometimes they kind of settle for just being okay, just being good.

A: Yes.

Q: When you know, just those little things; as you say, that little bit over and above; that little bit of extra care just speaks volumes doesn't it?

A: Yes. There's a great book about that, I don't know if you've read it Yvonne, called 'Good to Great'. I think it's by Jim Collins, 'Good to Great'. He basically says that, 'good is the enemy of great', because it's so easy to settle for being good enough, but when you're good enough you get complacent and then you don't go for the great because you're doing okay and you're getting a certain amount of customers. It puts you into the wrong mindset, whereas when you go for great and you're constantly innovating and wanting to be like 200 percent better than last year; it puts you into a completely different mindset around your business. It gets you thinking innovatively.

Thank you so much Rachel, thanks for your time.

Please do book your Free Consultation to see how you could find your niche and dramatically increase your income here: http://bedandbreakfastcoach.com/your-free-bonus/#

CHAPTER 5:   YOUR WEBSITE

Why do I need a website?

Well if you're like me and you started your B&B business before the arrival of the internet then you may be forgiven for thinking you don't need one or that it's just a shop window and that it can't do anything for you.

You may think that your guests are not online and won't look at your website. Nothing could be further from the truth. Let's take a look at some facts:

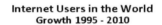

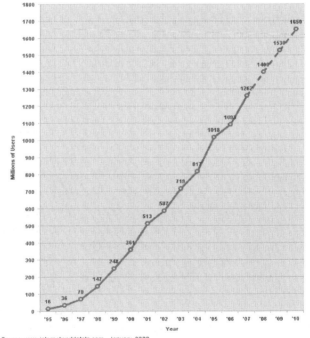

Source: www.internetworldstats.com - January, 2008
Copyright © 2008, Miniwatts Marketing Group

I think this chart demonstrates exactly why we need

to be online and looking good. But it's not just enough to be online; we have to have a compelling proposition for our visitors. And an easy way for them to buy from us and we'll look at that shortly.

Just because you don't surf the net, don't imagine that your potential guests don't. They do and the numbers are rising.

In fact I believe that the internet will be seen in the future as mankind's biggest connector, but that's just my opinion.

So how does the internet work?

The internet is like the platform where people can log into, go onto and find things, products and services; people and places that they are looking for. And if you are not there then you won't be found.

For example, when you go down your local high street and you are looking for a shoe shop for example, and there isn't a shoe shop there because they can't afford the rent or they've decided that they don't want to be in the high street; then they're never going to make a sale with you.

It's the same thing online, if you're not there, in the places where your guests are looking then you're not going to make any sales, you're not going to be found.

What are keywords and how do they work?

Well we couldn't talk about websites and the internet without talking about Google because they are closely linked.

So let me just explain how people find people online. Let's first imagine that your B&B is in a fishing village called 'Fishtown' in Scotland.

So let's also imagine that your potential guests come from Seattle in the USA and they've gone to Google to find some quality accommodation. They've already decided that they want to lodge in your area so they tap into Google something like this:

'Accommodations in Fishtown,'
'Accommodation in Fishtown,'
'Hotels in Fishtown,'
'Where to stay in Fishtown,'
'B&B's in Fishtown,'
'Luxury B&B's in Fishtown,'
'Guest houses in Fishtown,'
'Bed and Breakfasts in Fishtown.'

These are what we call keywords or keyword phrases.

Let's focus on the sequence of events. As they tap those keywords into Google, Google is now looking for websites that match those phrases. And it will bring up several that have those keywords embedded into their websites or something similar.

Google wants your potential guests to be matched up with you. They've been doing this very successfully for millions of people and businesses and many years now. And they're success rests on how well they match people up.

How do I get on page 1 of Google?

Doing some keyword research with the keyword tool that I mentioned earlier is the best way to find your keywords;

to find the people who are looking; tapping into the Google search engine what they are looking for and matching your website up with what they're looking for. And then producing lots and lots of content for your site on a regular basis using the keywords in the "optimization box" (don't worry, we'll get to that later) That's how you get onto page 1 of Google.

Now if you were to just use the keyword 'Scotland' for example, then you would be up against too much competition. So you need to have something much more specific. And the more specific you can get with your keyword phrase, using the Google keyword tool, means that you will be able to attract the people to your website much more easily because there will be less competition for those keywords.

What does 'Above the Fold' mean?

When designing your homepage of your website, your homepage is the first page that your potential guests see. And it's essential to be able to grab their attention immediately.

Statistics tell us that the average person makes up their mind as to whether the website they have come to will meet their needs in just seven seconds. So we have just seven seconds to make an impression.

So what you put "above the fold" to use a media-land expression, to make sure that you grab their attention in those crucial seven seconds is extremely important.

If you think of a newspaper folded in half you will notice that the sensationalist headline always appears on the top part of the fold and the rest of the story is below the fold. This is how newspapers grab our attention.

So taking that to our website design you want to let people know just what they need to know above the fold. So don't waste that space telling people about you and the awards you've won or worst still leave the space blank.

I'll move onto the essentials and non-essentials in that precious space in a moment, but for now take a look at your own website and try to see it from your potential guest's viewpoint. What would they like to know right up front? What would you want them to do when they land on your site? Hopefully you'll want them to book a room.

So what should I include on my homepage?

Let's talk about the essential elements for your homepage, what to leave in and what to leave out in that precious space above the fold.

First your banner. You'll want a professionally designed banner depicting exactly what your B&B is about. That means if your ideal guest is a fisherman and your B&B is in Fishtown in Scotland, then you'll want to have some images of fishing in your banner.

You'll also want to include some words. So the name of your B&B, "Fisherman's Lodge," for example, "Fishtown, Scotland." So people know exactly where you're situated.

If you love cooking and that's part of your offering then include some shots of your delicious food in your banner.

Next studies show that website visitors are naturally drawn to the right-hand-side for information. So in the top right of your above the fold space, you will need to let them know that they can check availability, look up your rates and connect and contact you.

Underneath your beautiful banner you'll need a navigation bar which should be no more than seven tabs. More than seven is too confusing and confused buyers never buy. Use drop-down menus if you have more to offer.

Essentials on your navigation bar are: Home; Rooms; Book Online Now; About; What's on in Fishtown; and Blog.

Underneath your navigation bar you'll need a slider, which is a moving image plug-in which shows images of your rooms and changes.

And finally above the fold on the right you'll need your social media button and your TripAdvisor badge, which reassure guests that your B&B is well liked. And that's all.

Now let's deal with the non-essentials.

What should I not include on my homepage?

Here's the mistakes that I see above the fold on the homepage.

A logo banner which says nothing at all about what they offer taking up valuable space above the fold.

Masses and masses of small text that takes ages to read through and only talks about the owners and their awards, rather than sparking the imagination of the potential guest and tempting them inside.

Bombarding visitors with everything on the front page. Your job is to give them a taster and invite them to look further keeping them on your site for longer, which means they're much more likely to book.

No online booking system. This is absolutely essential in today's world. Online booking means you can be booked by someone on the other side of the world while you're sleeping. It allows guests to book when they want, not when you want.

No social media button. Again in today's world it is absolutely essential to be on social media and I'll go into that in a bit more detail later on.

But the worst thing I see is blank white space. This area above the fold is your most valuable piece of real estate. Don't waste it and certainly don't leave it blank. In fact minimize the white space as much as possible. Keep your website neat and tidy.

And finally, no call to action. We want visitors to be inspired to book. Make it easy for them to do that as soon as they come to your site.

How else can I catch a potential guest when they visit but don't book?

Not everybody who visits will book a room straight away. Some people take longer to make up their minds. So rather than let them leave empty handed we can invite them to find out more about the local area, a little about us, by offering them our free guide. This is an essential piece of the puzzle for building what I call a *lead generation* system, which we'll get to later.

So you'll need a sign up box on the right hand side of your homepage, below the fold so that people can join your list.

To get your website found on Google, and in place for your ideal guests to find you online, using a WordPress website is hands down the best platform out there (at the time of writing). It is so easy and simple to use and allows us to "optmise" every single page or blog post.

I've already got a website so why do I need it to use WordPress?

You may indeed have spent a fortune on a custom built website or you may have got your daughter's best friend's brother to do it for you. I come across this a lot, but let me ask you this…. How is it working for you?. I recommend that all my mentoring clients switch their websites to WordPress, and I recommend that if you're not already on WordPress then you should be. Let me explain why.

Firstly it is really, really easy to optimize your site for the search engines, and that means easily sprinkling your site with the keywords that you've just discovered on the keyword research we did earlier.

Secondly it has the easiest to use admin system where we add pages, log post images, videos, and any other media that we want to use.

Thirdly, it has the widest collections of "plug-ins" I've ever seen. Whatever bit of functionality you want to improve or add you can find a WordPress plug-in, which means searching for it, installing it, and activating it. It's so simple.

Fourth, you don't need an experienced website programmer to do anything for you; you can do it all yourself, even if you're afraid of technology you will love WordPress.

So when you look at all those large hotel booking sites and marvel at all the imagery, moving pictures, videos and buttons, rest assured you can do all this yourself with a WordPress site for a fraction of the costs. You just need to be willing to learn how.

I work with Marion Ryan at http://onlinebusinessgym.com who builds fabulous WordPress websites and can move your site to WordPress very quickly and inexpensively. I recommend you check her out.

What are "plug-ins" and how do they work?

Plug-ins are little bits of functionality that you add to your WordPress website. They can range from doing things like having a moving picture slider image thing on your front page. They can have a call to action in your side bar. They can link your social media buttons to your own Facebook page or your LinkedIn profile, or your Twitter account. They can allow your visitors to share your information with other people by clicking on 'share' buttons.

They can do any kind of extra functionality on your website. They can link you to other sites; anything that you choose that you want to add to your basic site; you can usually find a plug-in for it. Another excellent plug-in is that you can link it into your site to Google Analytics, and I'll come to why that's important later on in the book.

What is SEO and why do I need to use it?

SEO, a much banded around phrase. What does it mean and how does it work? SEO means search engine optimization and here's how it works.

With our new list of keywords that we've just discovered via the Google keyword tool, we now need to sprinkle them all over our website. This is why I love WordPress because it easily allows you to do that, on every single page, on every single blog post you create on your site; you can put your keywords in it using the plug-in called: All-in-One SEO. You have the option to enter a title of your page which must include a keyword and then in the short description of your page or post you can then add another relevant keyword phrase.

And then finally, in the keywords box, you put some relevant keywords. I stress the word 'relevant' here. If you're posting or creating a page about a Car Boot Sale in Fishtown you won't want to use the keywords for wine tasting in Fishtown because Google won't match you with people looking for the Car Boot Sale.

Have you ever typed in some keywords into Google and then been offered several websites which have nothing to do with what you're looking for? Frustrating isn't it? Well don't be one of them.

How do I know if my website is working for me?

This is where Google Analytics comes in. You install the Google Analytics plug-in into your WordPress website and you get immediate access to statistics on who is visiting your site, where they're coming from, how long they're staying on your page, which page they're visiting that is most popular, which language they're using; and how many people visited your website every single day. This is vital information for marketing purposes. We need to know which blog post are proving the most popular; we need to know which pages are working, or which pages are visiting the most, so that we can target our marketing even more directly to the people who want what we have.

Google Analytics is absolutely vital to know how many visitors are coming to your site, how long they're staying, which pages they're checking on and which countries they're coming from.

Check out my own site at http://bedandbreakfastinchampagne.com to see how I have positioned essential information "above the fold" and notice that I've used keywords in my domain name (the web address) rather than the name of my B&B which is "Les Molyneux" because in the beginning when I first started to take control of my marketing, no-one was searching on "Les Molyneux" but from my keyword research, I knew that "bed and breakfast champagne" was a great keyword phrase and I wanted to have the best chance of being seen and picked up by Google, so I chose that keyword phrase as my domain name.

There's also a Home Page Website Template available for you to download at: http://bedandbreakfastcoach.com/your-free-bonuses/#

Action Steps:

- Take a look at your own website and see how much space you're wasting "above the fold"
- Read your text from your guests' point of view – is it tempting them inside, or are you just talking about you?
- Check to see if you have the essential elements in

place and how you could change it
- If you're not already on WordPress, then seriously think about moving

How does your website shape up? If you'd like to know for sure, then book your Free Consultation with me here: http://bedandbreakfastcoach.com/your-free-bonus/#

CHAPTER 6 : ONLINE TECHNOLOGY

What is online technology?

Online technology, in essence, is third party software that helps you to run your Bed & Breakfast business better. So that could be anything from Facebook, Twitter, LinkedIn, Trip Advisor, Booking.com, Customer Relationship Management system, Quick Books, Online Booking system, and email list managers. Those are just some of the third party software installations that come under the heading of Online Technology.

How has it changed our lives?

Well, online technology; and I think you'll probably agree, has changed our lives tremendously in the last few years. Do you remember the days when people used to phone up? In our house when the phone rang, everyone would scramble to answer it. It was such a novel experience. Nowadays, hardly anyone uses traditional phones, but uses text messaging on mobile phones instead. How much easier is it to keep in touch these days? It's so much easier than relying on one method of communication as we did in the age of traditional phones.

And what about video? Who would have thought that we'd be able to make fools of ourselves and put them out into the world for all to see? Who would have thought that we'd be talking into a computer and see the other person talking back to us?

And social media; who would have thought that we'd be able to keep up to date with what our friends and family are doing on a daily, hourly, or even minute basis?

It's incredible to think how far we've come in the last few years. I know that I marvel at the technology at our finger tips every single day. I know that many people are afraid of it; pass it off as a fad and refuse to get involved, but this is like saying, "I'm never going to drive one of those new fangled things called ' a car' when the horse and cart has done me just fine, thank you."

What disadvantages we create for ourselves when we adopt this attitude. Progress will keep on progressing regardless of what we think about it; and so we need to know how to apply this explosion in communication.

How has it changed our B&B businesses?

Back in the dark ages before the internet and the array of online technological solutions, we pretty much waited for the phone to ring, or for someone to knock on the door. It was all a little haphazard and uncertain wasn't it? But now we have the ability to attract guests from all over the world and have them reserve in advance, take deposits to reassure them that the room that they've booked we'll be there when they arrive.

Send them helpful information in advance for their stay, to help them plan a memorable experience with us, and also introduce more products and services that we offer; and all this can happen while we are sleeping or away doing something else. How cool is that? So let's break it down a little further.

We get reservations; we welcome guests; we give them a good time and we ask that they write in our guest book and they tell their friends and family; we invite them to visit us again.

The internet has just made it easier. The internet and

online technology has just made it easier to do all that. So instead of getting caught up in all the noise or worrying about what you aren't doing, let's just simplify it.

We get reservations, usually online now and if you're serious you already have an online booking system.

We welcome guests. Now we can welcome them before they even arrive with pre-prepared emails offering useful information about our B&B and our local area. And again if you're serious you've got this in place too.

We give them a good time. And because of the technology we're able to devote more time to our guests because the technology is doing the work for us. I hope you've got this set up too.

We ask that they write in our guest book and that they tell their friends and family. Instead of using the guest book we encourage them to write a review on TripAdvisor. So that it's not just their friends and family that can see us, but the whole world can. And this is a good thing.

We invite them to visit us again and again. Technology has made it even easier to do this. Nothing has really changed except for the way in which we do it.

Explain why I need an online booking system when most of my guests phone me?

Your online booking system should be taking full details of your incoming guests, like a deposit paid either directly into your bank account or into your PayPal account.

This not only helps with your own cashflow, meaning you get paid all year round, but reassures guests that their room is booked and available for them when they arrive at your B&B and they have the paperwork to prove it.

It also helps to keep your own system neat and tidy. If you are accepting reservations by telephone, email or even taking walk-ins, then keeping your records up to date is going to become a bit of a chore.

95% of my bookings come via my own booking system on my own website. Clearly guests prefer this method. So make sure you are offering this option whether you want it or not.

Even guests who telephone or email me to reserve are requested to use the online booking system, so that it automatically blocks off the booking and means I don't have to go into the system to update, which I may or may not forget to do. We are only human after all.

Another very good reason for using an online booking system is that you get more information about your guests which you can then upload into a database management system which we'll go into later.

So even if your guests are phoning you, it's because we haven't taken the trouble to educate them to use the online booking system.

Statistics show that this is the most preferred way to book accommodation now, online. So it's just a matter of education.

What is email marketing and why should I use it?

Email marketing via the internet has got a bit of a bad reputation in recent years. But believe it or not it's still the best form of marketing for your business.

Let's deal firstly with how it doesn't work. You have an Excel spreadsheet with all your contact details and you email them once a year from your Outlook, Gmail or Hotmail account.

Most of your emails bounce or only make it as far as the spam filters. This will not do I'm afraid.

First, it's illegal to do that. By law you must give people the option to unsubscribe from your list and to do that you need to be using professional List Manager such as Constant Contact, Aweber or the one I use which is Infusionsoft.

Infusionsoft is a fabulous piece of technology, not just for emailing and I'll come to that later.

If you're only emailing once a year to wish your past guests Happy Christmas then they will have completely forgotten who you are and quite possibly send you an unpleasant email complaining. Especially if there is no option to unsubscribe.

Your guests want to hear from you and email is the best way to keep in touch with your precious guests.

Now let's look at how emailing can properly work for you using some online technology.

What's a List Manager and how do I use it?

Let's go back to email marketing. 68% of people surveyed said they have made purchases online after receiving email. A special offer was the most compelling motivational factor for making an immediate purchase after clicking on an email.

Think about Amazon here. After you purchase something on Amazon they send you an email asking you what you thought about it and offer you something else. And how many times have you had a look and clicked on something else?

If your online booking software or your list management software does not allow you to send emails to guests who've booked then we need to add an email List Manager to our list of technological helpers for our B&B businesses.

Let me explain how it works.

Your guest books a room either by phone, in which case you need their email address taken over the phone; by email or through your booking system.

Step two is where we add enormous value to their experience before they even arrive and we do this using email List Manager with Auto Responders. Don't worry about the terminology I'll explain this later.

We need to be able to import their contact details but most importantly their names and email addresses into our system. We then need to have ready set-up a series of emails, preloaded into a list manager which about their visit and preps them for a truly memorable experience. These emails are called "Auto Responders."

What's an Auto Responder and how do I use it?

So taking my own system as an example. In the first email that is sent out from my List Manager with their contact details added, I include a link to my page on my website where I have recorded an introduction for guests.

In this video I introduce myself and thank them for their booking, reassuring them that their details will never be shared and inspiring them with what's possible for them when they visit us.

The Auto Responder is the sequence of emails that are triggered when I input the data. I also inform them that I will be sending more information through over the coming days and weeks, so to look out for it. So now they are expecting to hear from me with more wonderful things to see and do in my local area.

Do you see how powerful this is? Can you think of ways you could do something similar in your business?

There's more to cover on this topic, but this is really just to open your eyes to an easy automated way to start building the relationship with your guests.

What's a CRM system and why do I need one?

What you can do is you can start off on this path by just using a simple List Manager such as Aweber. A CRM system tells me everything about my guests. I'm able to tag them; I'm able to tell the system when they came; how long they stayed; what they ate for dinner; what their special dietary requirements are and where they live; what country they come from and all their contact details. I'm able to prep them for their visit; I'm able to take care of them before they even arrive.

The power of the CRM system is being able to segment your guests into people who came to stay in January; people who came to stay in March; people who came to July; whether they stayed one night; three nights; what they liked; what their preferences are so that we can target our marketing even more directly to our target guest.

How is communication with past guests going bring me more business?

When you've got that information at your fingertips you've got a really clear picture of your guests. You can then email them, your past guests and invite them to come back and stay with you again.

If they've had a lovely time and they've written a lovely review for you they will be only too happy to hear from you again with what else that you've got going on in your local area.

Don't forget they've already had a wonderful experience with you and studies show that it's much easier and much cheaper to sell to an existing customer than it is to go out and get a new one.

Capitalize on the goodwill that you've created between you and your guest to get them to come back again for another reason. Have some reasons at hand; have something regular to send out to your past guests so that they know that you're still thinking about them and that you still care about them.

What is blogging and why do I need to do that?

Here's some interesting information from socialexaminer.com.

"Over time a well fed blog will out-perform other blogs. This is evidenced by the impact of blog size on traffic and regeneration."

Note by 'blog size' I don't mean the size of the company but the number of blog posts accumulated over time.

Hotspot found that blogs that have accumulated at least 51 posts receive 53% more traffic than blogs with 20-50 posts. Additionally blogs with more than 100 posts see three times the traffic while those with over 200 posts see four and a half times the results.

This is amazing information about blogging. Your blog is a great place to showcase your local area. Armed with your video camera you can have a lot of fun filming local events; adding some of your own touches and takes on the event or just simply letting people into your life just a little.

If you don't want to use video and prefer to write then do what feels natural to you. However we always need to be thinking about adding value. Don't blog about stuff that doesn't matter to you, it will show through.

Blog only about subjects that interest you and are connected to your Bed & Breakfast business. For example, the other day I saw a post on Facebook with some pictures of gorgeous puppies. Now I just love dogs, so that immediately caught my eye. So I clicked on the link and spent a wonderful few minutes looking at pictures of the beautiful puppies on their blog and then of course commented on the Facebook page.

I'm sure that many other dog lovers did that too. And that that particular B&B got some enquiries from people who just wanted to come and see the puppies, which is perfect, because then they get to share your enthusiasm and passion for the puppies with likeminded people.

We couldn't do this 10 years ago, barely even five

years ago. So we must hop onto the trend and get involved or get left behind.

Blogging is a great way to keep connecting, improve your search engine ranking and be perceived as an expert. All of which ensure that potential guests choose you and your B&B over others in your area.

I'm confused about Social Media, how does it work for me and my B&B?

There's a lot of noise about Social Media. Let's just begin with Facebook. How does Facebook work?

With almost one billion users worldwide it's difficult to ignore this communication channel. But you'd be forgiven for assuming that Facebook is for youngsters. Take a look at this data directly from Facebook itself.

Social Networking Penetration Among Worldwide Demographic Groups

Source: comScore Media Metrix, Worldwide, October 2011 vs. July 2010

How does Facebook work?

First, let's take a look at the rise of Facebook users.

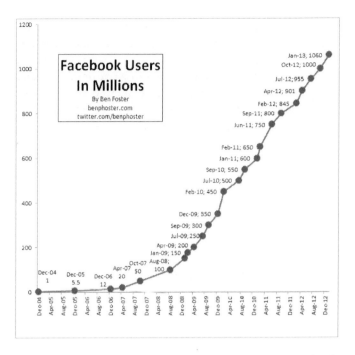

As the chart above illustrates the total US Facebook population is made up of millions of people across a range of age groups. While young adults, 18-25, lead the way with a combined 50 million users; almost double the size from a year ago. The 26-34 age group is now well behind with 29 million users.

And according to the data from Facebook there a combined 28 million people over the age of 45 are active on Facebook. These are impressive user numbers from an older demographic that continue to grow.

And it's important to note here that the 55-64 age group is almost the size of the 13-17 year old age group. Further evidence that Facebook isn't limited to young people.

Now that I've convinced you that Facebook is a necessary tool how do we go about leveraging Facebook for our businesses. First we must personally have a profile on Facebook. Then we create a page for our business. We add our own banner from our website or one of the most prominent pictures, but make sure that your Facebook page has the look and feel of your own website.

When you've got it set up invite your friends to "Like" you. When you've got at least 25 Likes you can then claim your name, which means that instead of the URL for your Facebook page being something like this https://www.facebook.com/LuhmoaxPhotography?sid=0.882481296949618

You can now customize it to look like this https://www.facebook.com/LesMolyneux

Link this page back to your own website via those Social Media buttons on the top right-hand-side that we talked about earlier on your website.

If your target market is on Facebook, then visit regularly and as a general rule post lots of personal and general things into it with something about your B&B on your personal profile. And post lots of stuff on your new page about your B&B and invite interaction.

Then you might want to consider highly targeted advertising.

How does LinkedIn work?

LinkedIn is a network of professional people. And depending on who you've identified as your target market you could use LinkedIn to find them.

For example I use LinkedIn extensively because my target market is champagne lovers. And when I did a search I found many groups dedicated to champagne, wine and wine tourism on LinkedIn.

Use the 'Search Groups' facility in the top right-hand corner of the Homepage on LinkedIn to search for groups around your topic and your target market.

Look and see what they're talking about, introduce yourself and what you do and then add value. Don't sell. There's nothing worse or more reputation destroying than having someone sell to you on the first date.

Get to know the movers and shakers or influences as they're called on LinkedIn and make friends, add value, offer to help. Add these people to your own network and when you add them tell them why you're adding them, such as, "I see we're members of the X group and I hope you will join my network.

Always type a personal message to invitations instead of leaving the standard message in place. It means you've taken the time to select that person and it makes them feel special.

Soon you'll have a sizeable network of likeminded people interested in what you do, all part of building your community online.

Make sure your profile is up to date and 100% complete on LinkedIn and that you've entered some of your keywords in your description of what you do and what you are. Don't make your profile all about you; make it about who you serve and what you offer.

How does Twitter work?

Twitter is a huge platform too. So let's take a look at these facts. Three hundred and forty million Tweets per day, 140 million users and rising. Every day millions of people turn to Twitter to connect to their interests; to share information and find out what's happening in the world right now.

Anyone can read, write and share messages of up to 140 characters on Twitter. These messages or Tweets are available to anyone interested in reading them whether logged in or not. Your followers receive one of your messages in their timeline, a feed of all the accounts they have subscribed to or followed on Twitter.

This unique combination of open public and unfiltered Tweets delivered in a simple, standardized, 140 character unit allows Twitter users to share and discover what's happening on any device in real time.

For businesses and brands, such as your B&B business, these conversations provide a rich canvas and a power context in which to connect your messages and your B&B to what people are talking about right now.

It's a canvas to telling engaging stories; for participating in cultural events; for broadcasting content; for connecting directly with consumers and for driving transactions.

Businesses can influence and participate in real-time conversations on Twitter to drive guests to your website. B&B businesses can also use Twitter to listen and gather marketing intelligence and insight.

This is a great place to do a search on your target audience and see what they say on Twitter and engage with what they're saying; follow them and have them follow you.

It's likely that people are already talking about your business; your area; your competitors on Twitter. So you need to be on there too, just to see if they're there.

But don't be fooled into thinking that you have to be on all of these platforms all at the same time. You absolutely do not.

Find out where your guests are hanging out most; find out where you can add the most value and just go there.

Think of it like this, Facebook, Twitter and LinkedIn, as parties. So you need to be thinking about what party are my potential guests at. And go to that party on and go frequently, add value.

I've heard bad stuff about TripAdvisor. Why do I need to pay attention to it?

People have mixed opinions about TripAdvisor.

Do you remember the good old days when people used to write lovely comments in our guest books? Other guests used to love flicking through the book to see what others had said and reading their comments; seeing where they were from etc.

The guest book was our primary source of guest experience but it was flawed wasn't it? Because the only people who got to see the comments were those who had already made the buying decision to stay with us i.e. the guests.

But now we have TripAdvisor, the world's largest

online review site attracting 40 million viewers a month and rising. This website allows anyone to post a comment about their experience at your B&B and your and others in your area are ranked according to how many comments are posted.

I know that many B&B owners do not like it, but trust me, I really do believe we can make it work for us if we go about it the right way.

It's true that we cannot control what people write about us. So we must first set an intention to be open to criticism and honesty.

There is always going to be someone who doesn't enjoy what we offer and that's okay. We must deal with it fairly, not defensively. Never ever get involved in a dispute with your guests.

So let's take a look at yet more statistics of the changes in human behavior brought about by the online technology.

78% of consumers trust peer recommendations.
Only 14% trust advertisements.
Only 18% of traditional TV campaigns generate a positive return on investment.

These figures are pretty clear. People trust people who are like themselves and they understand what they are saying on TripAdvisor is honest opinion and valuable feedback.

It's not going to go away, so rather than resisting let's decide to embrace it. So where do we start?

I highly recommend you set up a business account

with TripAdvisor which will cost you somewhere in the region of €30, £35, $50 a month at the time of writing. And this means that your B&B is now searchable again on another platform on the World Wide Web.

The way to get better rankings on TripAdvisor is to increase your reviews. How do we do that?

It goes without saying that we must give our guests a great experience, so they need to reciprocate with a glowing review and they will when they feel sufficiently cared about. The more care you give them the more the law of reciprocity will come into play.

The law of what, you ask? Think about it. When have you been given a gift at Christmas or even a card from someone unexpected and then quickly rummaged around to find something to send back. It's natural. So let it happen.

Second, interact with potential guests on the forum for your area offering advice, information and tips. This is a great place to build a reputation as the expert in your area. And soon people will be messaging you directly to ask for your help. You will become the trusted expert you need to be to increase your business and make more profit and have more fun.

Always add whatever you can but make sure it's of value. You don't need to contradict or get into disputes, that doesn't offer any value whatsoever. And most of all, do not sell.

Where do I find groups and forums?

On all of those Social Media platforms that I have just discussed there are groups and forums. On Twitter,

Facebook and LinkedIn there are search facilities on their sites.

But the very best place to go to find potential guests is on the travel forum in TripAdvisor.

On the TripAdvisor travel forums they are a great sources of inspiration for your own little book which we'll cover later.

People will be asking questions about your area and your niche and you can answer them and help them. Never promote your own Bed & Breakfast or your services as this will annoy others on the forum and ultimately TripAdvisor itself and you could get shut down.

Be as helpful as you can and give as much as you can and then you'll gain a reputation and people will click through to your profile. And then often they'll send you a message when they're ready to book with you.

Once you have your niche firmly decided upon then you can go out and look online for those people on those networks.

As local experts in our areas we are in a unique position to help people with their questions, problems and challenges.

The reviews will happen on TripAdvisor because guests who have come are already familiar with TripAdvisor so it's not necessary to explain how TripAdvisor works and how important it is for us, they already know.

Check out the travel forum for your local area and then dig down deep on the forum for where you can add the most value. Join the conversations.

I myself have found plenty of groups around the topic of champagne on LinkedIn, but you might find your target market hangs out on Facebook; you might find it hangs on out Twitter. Dig around using your keywords as your guide and see what you find making sure that you're not asking them to have sex with you on your first date, if you get my meaning. That means don't sell.

I don't know how to do videos, why should I bother?

A few specifics on YouTube first. YouTube sites have three billion views a day. According to Google's blog those three billion views represent a 50% increase over the last year.

"Nearly half the world's population is watching a YouTube video each day or every US resident watching at least nine videos a day," Google wrote.

Uploads have spiked as well. Over 48 hours of video are uploaded to the site every single minute. A 37% increase in the past six months and 100% increase on last year.

I find that quite amazing. Video is the future and if you're frightened of video; or you don't know how to do them then read on.

So people are looking for a connection everywhere, they want to feel special, respected and even loved. And we as B&B owners are in a unique position to fulfill their needs. We must step up to the mark and show them how much we do actually care because that really is the truth.

If you're like me you got into this business because you love homemaking, cooking, chatting, entertaining and meeting new people and you're good at it. The B&B experience is the perfect place to show off your skills.

And now the technology gives us greater opportunity than we ever had in the past thanks to YouTube, Webcam and videos.

Now I know that you may be thinking, "Heck I don't wanna be in front of a camera." And I'd like to ask you directly, "Why not?"

Maybe you think that being in front of the camera is like presenting on stage and again those statistics tell us that most people would rather die than do that.

In truth, speaking to the camera is much easier than in front of a crowd. If you stumble, you just start again. No one needs to see your outtakes. A really easy way on camera is to get a friend to interview you in a conversational way. You'll come across as relaxed and friendly, just what your future guests would like to see.

Of course if you're genuinely shy and that's rare for a B&B owner, then you might be surprised how easy it is for you to fix those nerves. Instead of focusing the camera on you, focus the camera on something that's going on in your local area and just talk, tell them what you're filming.

If you're not considering how video can help you boost your business then the chances are someone else is and they could be just down the road. Take a look at my blog and have a look at the videos that I've done in the past, just to give you an idea of where to start.

http://bedandbreakfastinchampagne.com/blog

And remember, each blog post or video blog can be

optimized with your keywords and add another piece of content to your website which Google can find. This will massively impact your website visitors, and therefore bookings.

Action Steps:

- For your videos and video blog, set yourself an account up with YouTube and buy yourself a small video camera, learn how to use it and start uploading some videos to YouTube. Just have some fun playing around. It pays to be yourself and a warm smile will be far more important than how eloquently you can speak.

- Auto Responders. If you're not using this already I urge you to investigate those I've mentioned and see which one you like. I use Infusionsoft myself but can wholeheartedly recommend Aweber for affordability and ease of use.

- Social Media Interaction. If you haven't already set yourself up with a Facebook Fan Page for your business and put lots of pictures on it. Again play around and have some fun. Set up a Twitter account too.   Find your groups online.

- Blogging, if you don't have this facility already add a blog to your site or get one at WordPress and practice writing some blogs.

- Reviews on TripAdvisor. Open a business account at TripAdvisor and post lots of photos there and start interacting on the forum sharing your knowledge. Your business account also allows you to order some small cards which you can give to your guests to remind them to write a review for you. This will massively increase your reviews, therefore your bookings.

Have you been avoiding learning about online technology? Find out more by booking your Free Consultation here: http://bedandbreakfastcoach.com/your-free-bonus/#

CHAPTER 7 : ADDING REVENUE STREAMS

Explain why I can't just sell Bed & Breakfast?

if you want to make 100,000 a year and still be able to take some time out regularly for yourself then you can't just sell rooms.

Imagine this, if your season is 26 weeks and you've got four rooms, then your availability is 728 rooms to sell. If you fill every room, every single night and your room rate is $100, then you'll make $72,800, but you'll be exhausted.

Why not sell half that number of rooms and make even more money with products and services for which you don't have to work so hard.

You'll be much better able to take care of your guests; you'll be relaxed; less stressed and more present for your guests, which is essential in a person-to-person business like a B&B business.

In 2012, 40% of my revenue came from other products and services I created around the needs, wants and desires of my guests.

When we focus just on occupancy rates we lose sight of the bigger picture where we can make more money for doing the same amount of work. And in some cases we can set up something once and get paid over and over with no extra work. But greater perceived value for our guests.
So how do I know what products and services to create?

Let's talk a little bit now of some of the things we can do, keeping in mind that we don't want to create another job for ourselves. We already have enough to do, but we do want to make more money.

Back in the days before the internet when we used to just sell rooms and the occasional dinner, it was difficult to offer anything else back then. But now things have changed and we can create all manner of digital products which you can sell online, taking money while we're sleeping or doing something else.

When we add additional revenue streams to our offering we open the way up to make more money and serve our guests in a much more expansive way. When guests choose a B&B over a hotel, they're looking for a personal experience; a chance to meet you; talk with you and get a little piece of you and your knowledge.

Think about it. How many times have you given directions to a little known place you know which has a great view; explained about a particular local attraction you know about; looked up the opening hours of a local museum; recommended a local restaurant; directed them to a specialty show you know; copied down a recipe? I bet you've done this over and over and over, just like I have.

This is the kind of information that your guests are looking for. The hidden gems; the secrets; the personal recommendations. In short, your take on things.

This is one of the reasons they choose a B&B over a hotel and we must deliver on that, we must meet their needs. And done properly we can charge for this.

Explain how packaging up my knowledge will make me more attractive and make more money?

When I thought about how many times I'd been asked for the same information and how many times I'd given it a light went on in my head. Why not produce my own local guide of this area?

Now you may say, "They can get the information at the local tourist office, so why would anyone want my guide." Not true.

As I explained earlier, guests want your take on things. Anyone can go to the local tourist office and get standard information, but your guests want your information; your knowledge; your recommendations; your secrets of the local area. They want the inside scoop that no one else knows. They want to feel like they're special and there's no one better placed to do that than you and your B&B.

How can we do that?

What is a digital product and why do I need to create one?

A digital product is a piece of content, like your free guide of your local area based on what we know hosted online that guests can download any time of the day or night whenever they wish.

So here's how it works. You make a note of all those recommendations you've made over the years. You put them into four or five categories and write some information around them. You put in a paragraph at the beginning about yourself and your B&B and why you're qualified to advise and make sure to put the link in which takes people directly to your website. Add some nice pictures and bingo you've just created your first digital product.

What do I need to include in the digital product?

Your own personal recommendations are what is needed in the digital product. You can choose; you can put in your local restaurants; you can put in the local attractions; you can put in anything that you like about your local area and where you know that your guests are going to get a good experience.

For example, in our own case we created a guide to Champagne. In the beginning it was a free guide and I'll explain to you how I made that into a paid guide later.

But to begin with it was a free guide. So we know that people come to here to discover the hidden gems of champagne. Anybody can rock up to the big champagne houses, pay to get in and take a standard tour around the cellars of the champagne houses. You don't need any particular expertise to do that.

But it's much more difficult to find a welcoming small champagne producer where they speak English and where they are prepared to welcome foreigners.

And so we know where these people are. So we packaged up that knowledge into our own free guide of the champagne region. We put in the pictures; we put in the contact details; we added little stories about the champagne producers. All the little things that people would never know about.

How do I sell them online and offline?

So once you've got your digital guide you need to make it into a PDF product and you need to upload it to your website. That's why WordPress is so wonderful because you can do it so easily.

Your digital guide needs to contain information about you because think about it? When this guide is distributed on the World Wide Web people might forget where they got it from. So in the footer it needs to have your website address, your name and your contact phone number. So that people know where they got this guide from and they know where they can get more information.

PDF it and upload it to your website and that will give you its own URL.

Now in order for people to get this guide, this is your tempter to get people into your community; to get onto your list even though they haven't yet booked a room. Because you can use this free guide as a lead generation tool to get people into your community and onto your list.

So the next thing we need to do is to setup your List Manager, setup your little sign-up box on your website and you need to promote your guide within that little sign-up box.

So as people enter their details, they're onto your list, they then get sent a series of Auto Response emails which we talked about earlier and in the first emails they get is the link, the URL where you just uploaded your digital product that takes them to that URL and they immediately get the guide.

So that is how you get your product online. Now what we did is we created this free guide in the beginning and then it became a paid guide and then it became an iphone/ipad App.

So how we did that, is we added even more

information. When I first produced my first guide about five years ago, it was only about three or five pages long. And then as the years went on I added to it every single year with new information; new people I wanted people to meet; new people who wanted business; new people that I discovered and the guide got bigger and bigger and it ended up being a 30 page e-book.

So then I decided to charge for that e-book. Now that is another product that is delivered to people with an offer to purchase it through my email Auto Responder service for people who have booked to come here.

The next stage I went to, is I made it into an App. It's the same information with lots of videos so people can really get a connection to the local people before they come to the area. This is a fantastic way of helping your local business community as well.

So people can advertise their services in our app called Champagne Day and you can get that at

https://itunes.apple.com/us/app/champagne-day/id500021506?ls=1&mt=8

People can download the app and it's just another way of having the same information.

So that's how you sell it, that's how you get it out into the hands of the people who want what you have.
How do I get people to actually pay for it?

You add value to it and you market it as an essential guide to your local area inviting people to discover people and places that they would never find on their own without you. So you're positioning yourself as the go-to person, the expert in your niche, in your local area for people who are visiting your area.

That's great, but what else could I do?

The next thing you can do is to create a special page uniquely for your free guide or your paid guide on your website.

Add a picture of it and add some text saying why this guide will be useful for potential visitors to your region. Add your sign-up box at the bottom, which will be directly linked to your List Manager so that you are collecting data legally.

Anyone who signs up will have to opt in, thereby making a choice to stay in touch with you.

Now you can start publicizing your new free guide or paid guide around the World Wide Web.

So what other revenue streams could I add?

You're probably already offering evening meals. If not you certainly could be. Even if you don't like cooking yourself, there's still a way for you to offer this service but without doing all the work.

Make meals part of the mix that you're offering for your target guests. Almost 90% of all of our guests take an evening meal.

We offer two levels of evening meals and almost everybody chooses the lower priced option, but that suits me. I've priced it just right for me to be able to make double that.

For my example, my two-course evening meal with champagne, wine, tea, coffee is priced currently at €35 per person. That means that as long as the meal itself doesn't cost me more than €17.5 then I'm making 100% profit, which is in line with my budget.

I'm careful to keep within the parameters by keeping accurate financial records which we've already discussed.

But here's the thing, I don't cook the meal myself. Even though I love cooking I don't need to add this to my job list. This was a mindset shift for me and I struggled with it at first.

I believed that guests wanted me to cook for them, but in fact that wasn't true. Instead, I use the services of a local chef and make a big fuss about him in my marketing. Having a French chef locally means I can help his business at the same time while giving my guests a taste of real authentic French cooking.

Guests love this and it works really, really well.

My target market is the international English speaking community who want to discover the hidden gems of champagne. This means that many of my guests have travelled long distances before they arrive. Sometimes they've been on the road for several days or weeks. Sometimes they're fed up with restaurant food, hotel service and expensive laundry services. And so I do step into the breach and fill this need too.

And this forms another small revenue stream. Remember that small streams make up a big river and the more small streams you can create the bigger the river and your overall income.

The guest laundry is done by my lovely cleaning ladies and we guarantee to have everything turned around within 48 hours, washed, dried and ironed and delivered to their rooms.

I explain that offering this service means that they will make more money and thereby help the local community which is central to my philosophy. Guests are more than happy to pay for the service and glad that they can contribute to the local economy too.

It really just depends on how you frame it as to their response. Make sure you're emphasising how much you're helping the local community and your team. This appeals to an invisible force within us which is that we all want to help others and make the world a better place.

When you connect people to that you'll have absolutely no problem.

Another little stream which helps make the river even bigger, is the opportunity to purchase picnic lunch. Once again I do not make the picnic; instead I use the lovely services of my local baker and delicatessen to assemble a delicious picnic lunch for my guests.

I offer a bottle of champagne too and package it up in a nice branded bag and off they go.

Sometimes I mark it with their names particularly if there are many people in the party. It's almost like an individually prepared meal for each person, making everyone feel special.

It's always a balance between the time taken for the special touch and the return on that investment. Make sure that you're not giving yourself too many small jobs that don't really add much value to your guests.

There will be many artisans in your local area who are just longing for people to appreciate their art, photography, jam, honey, handicrafts, quilting, crochet, woodwork, wine, books, postcards etc. etc.

How many people could you help in your local area. Use your imagination to find a way to stock their products without laying out money up front and then taking a commission on whatever you sell. Make sure you do sell though.

Keep in mind that people on holiday have money to spend and are often looking for that special souvenir to take back home. Put yourself in the firing line here and help them to choose something from your local area adding value to everyone concerned.

How much difference does this make to my overall profitability?

Small income streams add up to big income streams. So several little ones will add up to a big river.

So don't miss the fact that you only make a couple of hundred or a couple of thousand on something because it's all adding to the bottom line. But do be aware, do not make the job an extra job for you. Make sure that you can outsource it somehow, get someone else to do it or make sure that there is minimal call on your time for you to provide these extra services.

Last year my additional 7 revenue streams, apart from my rooms, made up 40% of my revenue.

Action Steps

- Commit to creating a Free Guide to your local area

- Install a List Manager to collect contact details of potential guests and build your database

- Automate the lead generation process as much as possible by getting good at using online technology

- Identify some local businesses whose products would be a good fit for your B&B guests

- Set up your social media accounts, find groups and start interacting with people online

- Set up a Trip Advisor business account and order your free cards to build your online reviews and get more bookings

I go into additional revenue streams in much more detail on your Free Consultation, so book your slot here now: http://bedandbreakfastcoach.com/your-free-bonus/#

CHAPTER 8 : PARTNERING

Why do I need to partner with other businesses?

When I set up my Bed & Breakfast many years ago I didn't really understand the concept of partnering. I thought that I just had to take care of myself and let everyone else worry about themselves. And this is probably true for most people'S thinking in the world today.

But here's the secret. When you take care of yourself and others then you're able to take more and more care of yourself.

Now how does this work. My personal philosophy is that my Bed & Breakfast business must serve the local community. I take care of the marketing which brings many guests to my B&B, I gain.

The more guests I attract the more bread and breakfast supplies I can buy at the local baker, they gain.

The more I upsell my guests to take dinner, the more meals I can order for my local chef, he gains.

The more guests I attract to whom I offer complimentary champagne, the more champagne I buy from our local producers, they gain.

The more guests I inform and educate about my local area the more other attractions gain. The more guests I attract and can't accommodate the more other B&B's in the local area gain.

Keep in mind that I don't ask for anything in return, but this virtuous cycle of goodwill and collaboration pays me back in many ways.

All of the people I help in my local community send me extra guests whenever they can because they understand how I operate and they know that when they win I will win.

I personally believe that if more businesses operated like this the world would look a lot different to how it looks right now.

How do I identify suitable partners?

Finding partners to work with is another key element to your Bed & Breakfast business. So it's a good idea to select your partners carefully.

Essentially you will be passing business to these partners, so we need to ensure that they are prepared to do something in return for you or your guests.

This can take the form of monetary remuneration or something else entirely. I suggest you interview your preferred partners to make sure first. Explain to them that you run a Bed & Breakfast in your town and that people who stay with you are often looking for their service and first of all ask them if they'd like any more business.

It sounds obvious that they would say, "Yes." But don't assume. Several years ago I used to send my guests to a particular champagne maker in our village. I hadn't bothered to interview him, I just assumed that they'd like more business.

They were a traditional French champagne family operating in our village for at least 200 years and provided quite an amusing take on champagne for my guests. Madame was usually in her nightdress with a coat over the top and Monsieur was usually in his slippers when the guests arrived.

After several months of what I thought of as helping them to sell more champagne, they phoned me to say, "Please don't send anyone else because we don't have any more champagne to sell."

As you can imagine this came as a real shock to me. But I learned then and there that we must always ask and don't assume anything.

Why do I need to focus on their businesses?

You might think that it's strange that I'm suggesting that you look for more ways to add values to someone else's business, but here's how it works.

My philosophy is, "Give to Get." And give first and keep giving. One of the ways you can help someone else's business is to write a short article for them and put it on your blog.

I talked about blogging already. And this is a very easy way to create content for your blog which gets you more references on Google which means that your site will be returned more times than, for example, another B&B site in your town when people search on your keywords.

This is really important. I've already talked about keywords.

If you wrote a blog post of around 250 words with a lovely picture of each of your partner businesses you'd have plenty of fresh content for your site and you will be promoting their businesses as well. These will in turn create a lot of goodwill for yourself and bring you more bookings.

They will probably be astonished when you suggest this to them because no one else has ever done anything for them before. So you will not only look good in their eyes, they will be much more open to do things for you.

It's the law of reciprocation again at work. Don't worry about how it works just know that it does. What you give out to the world will be returned to you tenfold. So go out and get giving. Offer to help and watch your own business explode.

How can I get my local restaurants to recommend me?

I recommend that you select around three to five local restaurants if possible. Go eat there and get to know the people who run the restaurants. You'll be sending your precious guests there so you want to make sure that they are worth patronizing.

Ask the proprietor to offer something free or special for your guests. One of the ways that we do this is that our preferred restaurant partners give out their business cards and we write on the back the name of our B&B, then they know that it's us who sent them customers. Then they reward our guests with a free glass of champagne, a complimentary first course, a coffee or a small discount on the entire meal. The choice is theirs.

At the end of the year one particular restaurant invites all of his partners to a complimentary dinner at the time of our choosing and so we are all rewarded for sending him more business.

It's a win, win, win for all concerned which is my

favorite way of doing business.

And the other benefit is that when he has the chance he sends guests to us knowing that we'll send them back to him to eat on another occasion. This is a very special way to support your local community.

How do I promote the local attractions in my area?

The very best way to discover what your area has to offer is to literally become a tourist for a while. Go out visiting your local attractions and get a feel for what they do and how they operate.

I have personally visited and experienced everyone I recommend and promote. And it was such a lot of fun exploring.

So what's going on in your area that would be interesting to your guests?

I know that most of my guests come to discover the hidden gems of champagne. So I visited all the large champagne houses and many smaller ones to find out their opening times and to get to know the people I would be phoning to make appointments for my guests.

If I didn't get a good feeling about them then I didn't include them in my preferred partner list.

You could do this work from the comfort of your desk, but I prefer to get out and meet people. Plus it's a great opportunity to touch base with your local area again. Sometimes we work too hard and forget to go out.

Not all my guests come for the champagne so I wanted to offer some alternatives for families, walkers, cyclists, historians etc.

Make a list now of the attractions in your area keeping in mind the wants and needs of your ideal guests and then set aside some time to go out and find out.

Action steps:

- Identify local partners you'd like to promote
- Visit them and experience their product or service first hand
- Set up a system so that they know that you are promoting them
- As them to do something special for your guests
- Remember to ask if they want more business first!

FINAL CHAPTER – LAST WORDS

In this book, you'll find the exact steps I took to grow my own B&B from almost nothing to 100k a year in less than 3 years. I hope that you will take this information and implement the steps to do the same for your own B&B.

Small businesses are the lifeblood of any economy, and so we need to step up to the mark and make our own businesses work for us and for our communities.

Thank you for purchasing this book. Please do take advantage of the bonus gift of a Free Consultation by going here: http://bedandbreakfastcoach.com/your-free-bonus/#

Please let me know how you have used this book and the bonuses to grow your business. If you need help with anything at all, please contact me at yvonne@bedandbreakfastcoach.com and let me know how I may assist you.

I look forward to hearing from you and to meeting you sometime soon.

Yvonne x

Yvonne Halling runs "Les Molyneux" Luxury Bed and Breakfast in the heart of the Champagne region of France, where she won a Certificate of Excellence from Trip Advisor. She turned her 10k a year "hobby" business into a professional 100k a year B&B business in less than 3 years, through a proven 10 step system which she now uses with other B&B owners.

She's the winner of the Infusionsoft Ultimate Marketer Contest Best in Class 2013, has written for the UK Bed and Breakfast Association, interviewed on http://brightideas.co and is a regular contributor to http://entrepreneursoul.com. http://webreserv.eu and http://thebandber.com   She's also a published author.

Printed in Great Britain
by Amazon.co.uk, Ltd.,
Marston Gate.